Table of Contents

Overview
Purpose

The purpose of **SRA Intervenciones tempranas de la lectura** is to provide intensive small-group instruction in order to develop phonemic awareness, phonetic decoding, reading fluency, and comprehension.

SRA Intervenciones tempranas de la lectura is a comprehensive reading intervention for struggling beginning readers that scaffolds elements of tasks initially beyond the student's ability, permitting the student to concentrate on and complete only those elements within their range of competence. Lessons are designed to scaffold new information in ways that allow students to assimilate and integrate the information into existing schema.

A typical lesson includes activities designed to do the following: promote phonemic awareness, provide practice sounding out decodable words composed of previously taught letter-sound correspondences, teach spelling strategies, and give students the opportunity to read and reread connected text composed of decodable and high-frequency words while applying simple, effective comprehension strategies.

In the beginning, lessons focus primarily on how to use the alphabetic principle quickly and efficiently as well as on reading connected text and reading for meaning. Later lessons emphasize decoding multisyllabic and irregular words, building reading fluency, and developing comprehension skills. As students master alphabetic elements, the text becomes more difficult but remains decodable. Comprehension strategies include explicit instruction in sequencing, making and verifying predictions, recognizing story grammar, activating prior knowledge, and identifying the main idea.

Use of Instructional Time

SRA Intervenciones tempranas de la lectura maximizes academic engagement by moving lessons along in a rapid manner with constant interchange between teacher and students. "Teacher talk" is kept to a minimum, and the phrases in teaching routines are used repeatedly. Students answer questions in unison, ensuring that each student practices all content rather than watching and listening as a peer responds to the teacher. In a typical routine, the teacher asks all students to respond to letters, words, or text in unison and then gives individual turns that allow each student to demonstrate ownership of the content. Students move quickly from activity to activity within each lesson. A typical lesson includes seven to ten short activities that encompass multiple strands of content, such as phonemic awareness, alphabetic decoding and encoding, text fluency, and comprehension strategies. The time dedicated to each activity varies according to the nature of the content; yet, reading activities requiring the most time are completed in less than ten minutes. A student with a short attention span is better able to stay focused on the task at hand when activities change frequently.

Presentation Techniques

SRA Intervenciones tempranas de la lectura helps achieve superior outcomes with students through the various presentation techniques for delivering instruction. For example, the small-group design for instruction, with the students sitting in a semicircle around the teacher, allows the teacher to more readily give directions, offer think time, and elicit student responses. Another presentation technique is maintaining a fast pace throughout the lesson and transitioning seamlessly from activity to activity within each lesson, moving as quickly as students within the group are able to progress. The objective is to keep students focused and engaged while providing daily opportunities for them to develop greater fluency in all aspects of reading and learning, including lexical retrieval, word reading, text reading, and word writing.

Clear and consistent visual and auditory cues are established to elicit responses from students. The teacher asks for group and individual responses throughout the lesson, consistently monitoring student responses and providing praise for correct responses and immediate corrective feedback for errors. It is important to try to maintain a ratio of four praise points for every one correction. The teacher must make on-the-spot judgments about why errors occur and must focus on that aspect of the task when providing corrective feedback. The goal is to create a classroom based on positive feedback and support for students.

To enhance students' enthusiasm for learning, provide immediate and positive feedback for each activity as students demonstrate mastery. The Mastery Sheet lists each activity within each lesson. Place a check mark on the Mastery Sheet at the end of each activity while praising students. When all the activities in a lesson are mastered, place a sticker on the Mastery Sheet for that lesson.

SRA Intervenciones tempranas de la lectura defines mastery as 100 percent performance accuracy by every student, every day, on every activity. An important task is to determine when mastery has been achieved. Because the curriculum is designed to gradually and cumulatively become more complex, the majority of each lesson is composed of review and generalization work; each lesson has a mixture of review and new material. Thus, if mastery has been achieved on previous lessons, students should easily achieve mastery on new lessons. The expectation is that students begin each new activity ready to achieve at least 80 percent accuracy on their first try, with 100 percent accuracy after error corrections and scaffolding have occurred. Students demonstrate mastery during individual turns. If an error occurs during individual practice, the teacher will provide additional instruction and additional group practice, followed by another round of individual practice. Repeat this process until all students can perform the task without errors. If a particular task proves to be very difficult for a group of students, move on to another activity, but return to the difficult task later in the same lesson or on the following day. If the activity includes a reading fluency goal, it might be necessary to reteach several activities leading up to the story to achieve the fluency goal.

Introduction to the Curriculum

Student Objectives

Each activity is designed to support the following objectives.

1. Student ability to read and write letter-sound correspondences will be improved by attaining mastery in the daily letter-sound introduction and review activities. The most frequently encountered letters, such as *m, s, a,* and *t,* are introduced first, and the less frequent letters, such as *z* and *x* are introduced later.

2. Students will participate in a variety of activities designed to improve their phonological awareness skills. These activities include listening for sounds within words, playing the Pulgares hacia arriba o abajo (Thumbs Up—Thumbs Down) sound position game, and participating in stretching and blending activities.

3. Students will participate in activities that provide a strategy for decoding words. When they have mastered enough letter-sounds, students will sound out and read words in list form. These words are composed of the letter-sound correspondences students have mastered thus far.

4. Student ability to identify high-frequency words will be improved by continuous practice and review.

5. When enough letter-sound correspondences and high-frequency words have been mastered, students will begin to read decodable text using the strategies they have learned for sounding out words. You will provide guided practice and immediate feedback during each reading. To improve and increase reading accuracy and fluency, students will reread passages as an integral part of the reading process.

6. Students will learn a variety of reading comprehension strategies, such as how to make and verify a prediction, how to use sequencing strategies, how to draw conclusions, how to summarize key concepts, how to activate prior knowledge, and how to identify main events. You will lead these activities by asking the appropriate questions and eliciting relevant responses from the students as directed in the lessons.

7. To ensure that students are building toward the reading rate goal of an average first grader, fluency practice is built into the daily reading activity. Starting with an expected rate of 20 words per minute (WPM), students work toward a goal of 60 WPM by the end of **Teacher's Edition C.**

Student Benefits

Struggling readers must have help in order to gain proficiency in areas critical for building reading success. The *SRA Intervenciones tempranas de la lectura* curriculum for struggling readers provides carefully designed and integrated instruction and incorporates practice in critical reading skills to help students reach mastery level. Instruction includes phonemic awareness, letter-sound correspondences, word recognition and spelling, fluency, and comprehension strategies.

All reading activities are designed to promote success for even the lowest-performing readers. *SRA Intervenciones tempranas de la lectura* is highly motivational to struggling readers. Instruction and error-correction techniques are designed to enable and motivate all students to become better readers. Systematic review of previously learned material is provided in every lesson in order to promote mastery in content areas, and maximum reading time is built in to develop reading fluency.

Without effective and early intervention, struggling readers will fall farther and farther behind their peers. The *SRA Intervenciones tempranas de la lectura* curriculum provides the critical content and clear instruction needed to transform a struggling reader into a skilled reader. Results from multiple research studies confirm that after participating in this program for one year, more than 99% of students read at or above grade level.

Motivation

SRA Intervenciones tempranas de la lectura is designed to ensure few student errors and to provide every student with the best opportunity to succeed. Lessons are structured so that students go through a constant cycle of instruction, application, and review. As the teacher, you model each skill before requiring students to perform that skill. The activities are usually performed first in unison and then individually, until each student demonstrates ownership over the skill. In this way, students make few errors and feel competent.

Working toward mastery builds a sense of confidence and success in students. Getting the answer right is very reinforcing because students feel very smart! Consistently achieving mastery develops intrinsic motivation, instilling the desire within students to learn and achieve. Students are motivated to learn new material because they know they will soon be given the opportunity to apply what they have learned to another activity, thus demonstrating their mastery. The opportunity to successfully apply newly learned material is rewarding to students.

With *SRA Intervenciones tempranas de la lectura,* praise and tangible rewards provide additional sources of motivation for students. Praise should be genuine and frequent and should be given immediately after the response being recognized. Praise should be specific and relevant to the task at hand, offering useful information to the student, for example, **"Leyeron muy bien esta palabra, sonido por sonido." ("You read this word very well, one sound at a time.")** Students then know what they did correctly and how they did it correctly, so that they can apply that information to the next task to achieve success again.

Tangible rewards include the use of check marks and stickers on the Mastery Sheet. It is important to give check marks and stickers only when students have achieved mastery. Students are very aware of this system and will work hard to earn the rewards.

Your level of enthusiasm when presenting the materials is another primary source of motivation. This enthusiasm engages students from the very beginning and infuses them with a feeling of anticipation and excitement about what they are about to learn. You are encouraged to enjoy students' successes with them and let them know that you believe in them.

Each week students receive a Hora de Brillar (Time to Shine) Certificate to take home that relates information to families about what students have learned that week. This also allows the parents to get involved and show their excitement for, and interest in, their children's accomplishments, which provides additional motivation to succeed.

Skilled Readers Versus Struggling Readers

Skilled readers rapidly read words letter by letter. Their phonological processing of words is rapid and automatic. They are able to apply decoding skills, such as looking for smaller syllables within unknown words. Skilled readers use context clues to confirm that a word is pronounced correctly and makes sense. Skilled readers do *not* use context to decode unknown words.

Turning struggling readers into skilled readers requires daily, explicit, and systematic instruction that focuses on critical content. In particular, these students need to become efficient at using alphabetic information to decode unknown words and to build automatic word recognition, which in turn will facilitate fluency and comprehension. Instruction becomes cumulatively more difficult as the year progresses. Advanced skills are broken down into more manageable steps to enable student learning. Students need to achieve and experience success every day. This sense of achievement directly impacts their willingness to learn new material and to take chances in applying mastered skills in new situations. For this reason, progress is carefully monitored. Students receive constant and immediate feedback, through which they are provided with information that lets them know what they are doing correctly and how they are doing it, so they can continue applying mastered skills. Since each skill builds upon the previous one, all lessons are taught to mastery to ensure that students are able to handle each new skill before learning another.

Proof of Success

SRA Intervenciones tempranas de la lectura was designed and developed by reading experts conducting research on the prevention of reading failure. The program has proven to be effective as an intervention for at-risk readers in several large-scale studies. The curriculum has since been used as the primary intervention in studies involving second-language learners. In these studies, students who participated in *SRA Intervenciones tempranas de la lectura* made reading gains much greater than expected.

Intervention Basics

The instruction is designed for small groups of three to five students. A trained intervention teacher meets with students for sessions of forty minutes a day, five days a week. The instruction is explicit and systematic in presentation. A typical lesson can be completely taught in a forty-minute session. Depending on how quickly students master the activities, you can increase the pace of the lesson, or in some cases, slow the pace. At the instructor's discretion, students are paced through a lesson at the fastest rate at which they can achieve and maintain mastery. Since the lessons are cumulative and build on one another, it is essential that each lesson be mastered before moving on to the next lesson.

Because students are receiving reading instruction in both the classroom and in the intervention, they receive a double dose of reading. This approach creates an optimal situation for students to reach their grade level in reading and to have a real chance of catching up to their peers.

Materials

CURRICULUM MATERIALS
(Program-Provided)

- Ediciónes del maestro A, B, C (Teacher's Editions)
- Libros de actividades A, B, C (Activity Books)
- Answer Key
- Libros decodificables (Decodable Books)
- Libros decodificables Take-Home BLM
- Edición del estudiante (Student Edition)
- Tarjetas de sonidos (Sound Cards)
- Tarjetas de palabras de uso frecuente (High-Frequency Word Cards)
- Tarjetas de sílabas (Syllable Cards)
- Placement and Assessment Guide (includes Mastery Sheets)
- Staff Development Guide
- El muñeco Pepe (puppet)
- Teaching Tutor (available online only)

OTHER MATERIALS
(Teacher-Supplied)

- Timer
- Marker Board, Marker, and Eraser
- Easel
- Chart paper
- Stickers
- Pencils

Curriculum materials include three **Ediciones del maestro (Teacher's Editions)** and three **Libros de actividades (Activity Books)** for a total of 120 lessons. The list of curriculum materials helps to illustrate the variety of activities that contribute to making **SRA Intervenciones tempranas de la lectura** a comprehensive curriculum. You will need the second list of materials in addition to those provided by the **SRA Intervenciones tempranas de la lectura** curriculum. These materials guide you in providing the instruction struggling readers need in order to grow in ability, to stay on task, and to become skilled readers.

SRA Intervenciones tempranas de la lectura: An Integrated Curriculum

The *SRA Intervenciones tempranas de la lectura* curriculum is designed so that multiple strands are incorporated into all lessons. Although strands are presented separately in this guide for clarity, each strand is interwoven with the others to create a cumulative effect. The parallel strands contain skills that are embedded in more advanced skills, until each student has mastered the strand. Over the course of the intervention, as the strands are mastered, they collapse into one another until students are on grade level and can maintain successful reading growth.

Curriculum Strands

School Year
............................➤
Phonemic Awareness
............................➤
Letter-Sound Correspondences
............................➤
Word Recognition and Spelling
............................➤
Fluency
............................➤
Comprehension Strategies

Characteristics of Daily Lessons

Instruction is sequenced, and all elements are integrated. Each lesson consists of multiple strands and the skills used to teach those strands. The amount of new information introduced in any one lesson is kept to a minimum to help students as they assimilate only the immediate information. Most of each lesson is review and practice.

Classroom Arrangement

Each student needs to clearly see the **Teacher's Edition** and your cues during instruction. Students need to be close enough to you to hear all instructions. Students will also need an adequate amount of space at the table to complete writing tasks in the **Activity Books.**

You should sit so that all students can be seen clearly and so students' responses can be heard clearly. All students need to be monitored constantly and should be in easy arm's reach so that you can assist them during writing activities.

Throughout the lessons there are activities in which you will need to quickly turn to the side and write on the marker board. When you model the writing of a letter for letter-sound introduction or to correct an error during letter-writing and letter-sound dictation activities, you will use the marker board. In the Word Recognition and Spelling strand you will write on the board words with added endings for your students to read. In some comprehension activities you will be instructed to write student responses on either a large pad of paper or a board. Whatever you use needs to be within easy reaching distance from your seat. You do not want to have to move away from your chair or turn your back to the students when you are writing on the board. A medium-size marker board on an easel sitting to your side works very well for this.

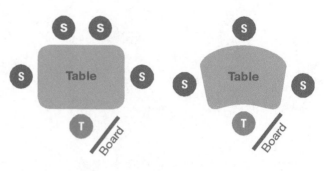

Students sit in a semicircle facing the teacher.

Strand Contents

As an integrated curriculum, the program provides an efficient framework for teaching students to read. Rather than being taught in isolation, one skill at a time, multiple strands are taught in unison on a daily basis, and each strand is interrelated with the next. This design adds an element of relevancy that increases the effectiveness of the instruction.

PHONEMIC AWARENESS

- Sound Discrimination
- Oral Blending
- Stretching
- Stretch and Blend

LETTER-SOUND CORRESPONDENCES

New and Review
- Introduction
- Writing
- Review
- Dictation

FLUENCY

- Connected Text
- Story-Time Readers
- Fluency Goals
- Partner Reading

WORD RECOGNITION AND SPELLING

- Sounding Out
- Reading Fast
- High Frequency Words
- Stretch and Spell
- Chunking/Multisyllabic Words

COMPREHENSION STRATEGIES

- Predict
- Retell
- Sequencing
- Story Grammar
- Sentence Completion
- Content Web
- Vocabulary Building
- What Did We Know?/What Did We Learn?
- Making Inferences
- Main ideas

Scope and Sequence

A scope and sequence chart can be found in the back of each **Teacher's Edition.** This chart allows you to see at a glance which instructional strands are being taught in a given lesson and the skills being taught for the strands. To practice reading the scope and sequence chart, locate the first lesson in the chart. Run your finger across the row following the numeral 1 to see which specific skills are taught in the first lesson of the intervention. To identify the strand for each skill, look for the strand name at the top of the column. For example, answering literal questions is a skill that is used to teach comprehension in the first lesson.

SCOPE AND SEQUENCE

Lesson Introduced	Phonemic Awareness	Letter-Sound Correspondences	Word Recognition and Spelling		Fluency	Comprehension Strategies
			Syllables	High-Frequency Words		
1	• Initial Sound • Building Syllables	• Mm				
2	• Building Syllables			• me		
3	• Initial Sound	• Aa				
4	• Building Syllables • Initial Sound • Last Sound					
5		• Accented Letters		• Él		
6	• Initial Sound • Last Sound	• Ss		• él		
7	• Building Syllables			• mi	• Connected Text	
8	• Initial Sound • Last Sound	• Ll				
9	• Building Syllables					
10	• Building Syllables			• ve		
11	• Initial Sound • Middle Sound • Building Syllables	• Pp				
12	• Initial Sound • Middle Sound			• en		
13	• Building Syllables • Initial Sound	• Nn	• ma • pa • sa • la			
14			• na	• es • esta	• Decodable Book 1, *Lala*	• Story Prediction

Appendix 1 Scope and Sequence

Staff Development Guide, Spanish

Fully Specified Lessons

The lesson dialogues in the **Teacher's Editions** act as a guide for the teacher. They are prescriptive and highly detailed, and they spell out every aspect of each activity. Each lesson is designed to communicate only what the students need to learn that particular day. Teaching formats are presented in clear and consistent language, and they have been thoroughly tested to ensure success.

Routines

Using consistent formats reduces student confusion and enhances student learning. The formats are specific to the different strands. As students master skills, the formats evolve over time to accommodate students' continual progression toward becoming successful and fluent readers. By planning each lesson ahead of time, instruction is consistently clear, and guesswork on the part of students is reduced. The overarching teaching routine repeated throughout the curriculum is composed of the following steps: modeling new content, providing guided practice, and implementing individual practice in every activity. Preview and prepare for each lesson before its presentation to be clear about what is expected of both you and students in each activity.

Format Presentation

The lesson dialogues include what you say, what the correct student response is, and how you should respond based on the accuracy of student responses. Present lessons in a natural way, without necessarily reading the dialogue word by word. You may slightly alter the wording, as long as you preserve the intended specific instructional goal of each activity. Try to maintain eye contact with your students throughout the lesson presentation.

A sample activity is displayed below. As you review the sample activity, you will see that the **Teacher's Editions** use three different typefaces so you can easily recognize each part of the activity at a glance:

Bold blue type indicates what you say.

Bold red type indicates what the students say.

(*Italic blue type in parentheses indicates what you do.*)

Look at the sample activity.

Look for dialogue that is written in bold blue type: **Ahora van a leer palabras sonido por sonido.** This is what you say to your students.

Look for dialogue that is written in bold red type: **/mmm/aaa/sss/aaa/.** This is the correct answer that you want to hear from your students. If you don't get the correct answer, then you will need to provide an error correction. Specific error corrections are discussed later in this guide.

Look for dialogue that is written in blue and italics: *(Slide your finger under each letter.)* This is what you do. Any necessary cues appear in blue and italics also. You may be asked to model a skill for students. These directions will vary from activity to activity, but they will be written in italic type also so that you will know at a glance what you are supposed to do.

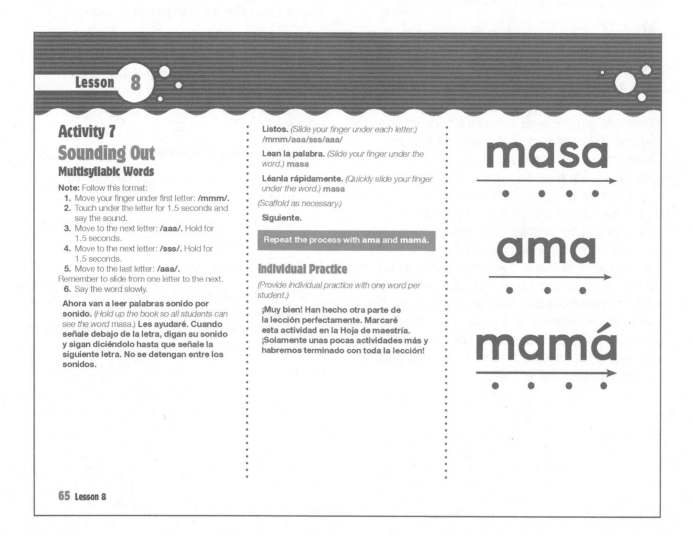

Lesson 8

Activity 7
Sounding Out
Multisyllabic Words

Note: Follow this format:
1. Move your finger under first letter: **/mmm/.**
2. Touch under the letter for 1.5 seconds and say the sound.
3. Move to the next letter: **/aaa/.** Hold for 1.5 seconds.
4. Move to the next letter: **/sss/.** Hold for 1.5 seconds.
5. Move to the last letter: **/aaa/.**
Remember to slide from one letter to the next.
6. Say the word slowly.

Ahora van a leer palabras sonido por sonido. *(Hold up the book so all students can see the word* masa.*) **Les ayudaré. Cuando señale debajo de la letra, digan su sonido y sigan diciéndolo hasta que señale la siguiente letra. No se detengan entre los sonidos.**

Listos. *(Slide your finger under each letter.)* /mmm/aaa/sss/aaa/

Lean la palabra. *(Slide your finger under the word.)* masa

Léanla rápidamente. *(Quickly slide your finger under the word.)* masa

(Scaffold as necessary.)

Siguiente.

Repeat the process with **ama** and **mamá**.

Individual Practice

(Provide individual practice with one word per student.)

¡Muy bien! Han hecho otra parte de la lección perfectamente. Marcaré esta actividad en la Hoja de maestría. ¡Solamente unas pocas actividades más y habremos terminado con toda la lección!

masa

ama

mamá

65 Lesson 8

Activity Tracking Chart

An activity tracking chart is located in the appendix of each **Teacher's Edition.** This chart allows you to see where each specific skill or concept is introduced and taught within the curriculum. For instance, as shown in the chart below, in Lessons 1–10 the letter-sound correspondences *Mm, Aa, Tt, Ss,* and *Rr* will be introduced and reviewed.

SRA **Intervenciones tempranas de la lectura**

	**ACTIVITY TRACK: Edición del maestro A, Lecciones 1–40**										
Lesson	Letter-Sound (New/Review)	Sound Discrimination/ Position	Stretching	Oral Blending	Write Letters/ Spell Words	Syllables	Sounding Out/ Multisyllabic Words	Reading Fast First	High- Frequency Words	Fluency	Comprehension Strategies
1	• Mm	• Beginning Sounds	★	★	★	★	★				
2	• Review			★	★	★	★		• me		
3	• Aa • Review	• Beginning Sounds	★	★	★						
4	• Review	• Beginning Sounds • Ending Sounds		★	★	★	★				
5	• Accented Letters • Review		★	★	★		★		• Él		
6	• Ss • Review	• Beginning Sounds • Ending Sounds	★		★		★		• él • Review		
7	• Review		★		★	★	★		• mi • Review	• Connected Text	
8	• Ll • Review	• Beginning Sounds • Ending Sounds			★	★	★		• Review	• Connected Text	
9	• Review			★	★	★	★			• Connected Text	
10			★		★	★	★		• ve • Review	• Connected Text	
11	• Pp • Review	• Beginning Sounds • Middle Sounds	★		★	★	★		• Review	• Connected Text	
12	• Review	• Beginning Sounds • Middle Sounds	★		★		★		• en • Review	• Connected Text	

Appendix 10 Activity Track Chart

Critical Features

There are three critical features for successful implementation of the materials: pacing, error correction, and teaching to mastery. All three must be present to achieve the level of success possible with the program. A well-paced lesson promotes the development of fluency and retention. Students are provided every minute of instruction with many opportunities to respond, ensuring that each student gets enough practice with concepts and skills to gain ownership of the practiced content.

Pacing

Instructional Pacing

Instructional pacing is a critical factor in the presentation of these lessons and can make or break the effectiveness of instruction. The objective is to go as fast as the students can go, without going faster than they can handle. In a well-paced lesson the dialogue between you and the students occurs as a rapid interchange. Fast pacing greatly increases academic engagement because students pay closer attention to the material being presented, which, in turn, increases learning by reducing behavior problems and keeping students involved and on task.

Good Pacing

Pacing should be fast enough to keep students attending and on task, but not so fast that they begin to guess and make errors. Pacing should be rapid. When students respond correctly, move quickly to the next instance or task. There should be minimal extraneous language—from you or the students—or off-task behavior during transitions. With good pacing, you will be able to elicit eight to ten responses per minute from each student! If the pacing is appropriate, students receive more practice time and have an increased opportunity for achieving success.

Ensuring Academic Responses with Cues

To achieve good pacing, you use a variety of cues. A cue indicates when students answer. Cues used to elicit student responses are either visual or auditory.

- Visual cues are used when the students are looking at you or at the **Teacher's Edition.**
- Auditory cues are used when the students are working from their **Activity Books** or reading from the **Decodables.**

Using cues helps you control pacing and provide appropriate think time for students before they answer. The use of cues minimizes students' tendency to guess or blurt out incorrect answers when they do not take time to think before answering.

The basic routine of each activity includes unison responses followed by individual practice. Students feel safer when answering in unison. Unison responses provide maximum opportunity for students to practice each skill as it is being taught. Cueing is an effective technique for keeping students together and for increasing automaticity of response.

Different formats require different cues. Be consistent to help students learn which cue is associated with each of the skills. Clarity of cues is essential to ensure that you move smoothly through tasks during instructional time. You will quickly find the cues that work best with your teaching style. The key is to be consistent with the cues and to keep them crisp and quick.

TYPES OF CUES

STRAND	RECOMMENDED CUE
All strands	**Hand Drop:** Cue is used to ensure that students will think before they provide an answer to a question. It can be used to elicit individual or unison responses. **Implementation of cue:** As you ask a question, hold your hand at shoulder level with your palm facing outward. Give approximately two seconds of think time, and then drop your hand with a slashing motion indicating that you are ready for the students' answer.
Phonemic Awareness	**First Sound:** Cue enables students to identify the first sound they hear within a word. **Implementation of cue:** Hold your right fist at shoulder level so the back of your hand is facing the students. Raise your index finger, cueing students to say the sound while reinforcing left-to-right directionality.
Phonemic Awareness	**Stretching Words:** Cue enables students to identify each sound they hear within a word. **Implementation of cue:** Hold your right fist at shoulder level so the back of your hand is facing the students, and hold up one finger for each sound within a word.
Letter-Sound Correspondences	**Point-Touch:** Cue guides students as they say each sound in a letter-sound review activity. **Implementation of cue:** Point to the letter-sound, pause, and touch under the letter-sound for students to read. Students say the sound as you touch under each letter-sound. Students hold the sound for as long as you touch under the letter or letter combination. Hold your finger under the letter-sound for two to three seconds for continuous sounds; touch quickly under stop sounds.
Word Recognition and Spelling	**Sounding Out/Read It:** Cue guides students as they read words. **Implementation of cue:** When having students sound out words, use the point-touch cue as described above, moving from left to right underneath the word. Guide students as they read the word by quickly sliding your finger under the word, moving from left to right.
Fluency	**Text Pacing:** This cue is used when students read the title of a reading selection in unison. **Implementation of cue:** Softly tap your finger or the eraser end of a pencil on the table for each word you want students to read. The rhythm should resemble that of a metronome, softly tapping at intervals of every two to three seconds or at a pace listed in the dialogue for the reading activity.

You will establish four rules from the very beginning to prepare students to observe and to respond properly to cueing: Sit tall; Listen big; Answer when I cue; and Answer together. A quick reminder is inserted in lesson presentation dialogues whenever necessary.

Error Corrections

It is important to give immediate corrective feedback to your students when they make an error. This means all errors are corrected as soon as they occur.

Error Correction: Basic Facts

A "basic fact" is anything that has no steps to achieving an answer and has only one right answer. Basic facts include naming letter-sound correspondences, identifying the first sound of a word, and automatically reading irregular sight words.

When an error occurs on a basic fact, model the fact by telling the fact: **Mi turno. El sonido de la letra es /sss/.** When you model, you literally do the task for the students, showing them how the task is done. Next, you ask *all* the students to repeat the item: **Ahora, ustedes juntos.** Last, you back up a few items and restart the activity: **Ahora, vamos a hacerlo otra vez.** By backing up one to two items, you are letting a little time pass between the correcting technique and retesting the group and/or the student on it. Error corrections are taught to the entire group, regardless of which student committed the error. This prevents confusion and allows all students to practice the correct response again. The lesson continues to move smoothly, and all students remain engaged.

Error Correction: Complex Tasks

When tasks have multiple steps, a "lead step" is added to the correction procedure. Examples of complex tasks include stretching and blending, segmenting a word into separate phonemes and then blending it back together, and sounding out a word and then reading it fast.

When an error is made on a complex task, first model the correct answer: **Mi turno.** Then lead the students: **Háganlo conmigo.** Then test students on the same item again: **Ahora, ustedes juntos.** Finally, back up one to two items and restart the activity: **Ahora, vamos a hacerlo otra vez.**

ERROR CORRECTION TECHNIQUES

Procedure 1:	Procedure 2:
Model: **Mi turno.**	Model: **Mi turno.**
Lead: **Háganlo conmigo.**	Test: **Ahora, ustedes juntos.**
Test: **Ahora, ustedes juntos.**	Retest: **Ahora, vamos a hacerlo otra vez.**
Retest: **Ahora, vamos a hacerlo otra vez.**	

Scaffolding

As students advance, you will not always want to model an entire series of steps when an error occurs on a complex task. Instead, you will provide scaffolding, leading students to use what they know to determine the correct answer without totally depending on you. Scaffolding requires on-the-spot teacher judgment. When you scaffold, you determine what piece of knowledge is needed to move the student to the correct answer.

For example, suppose that during letter-sound dictation activities, a student spells incorrectly the word *llama* with *y* at the beginning. You would remind the student that there is more than one way to spell the /y/ sound. You would then ask the student for another way to spell /y/. If at this point the student cannot remember the variant spelling, then revert to a more direct error correction technique. Show the student the correct letter-sound card for that sound-spelling, and have the student make the necessary correction. There is not one right way, so scaffolding depends on good judgment from the teacher. When in doubt, use the Model-Lead-Test correction technique.

Mastery

Every activity in every lesson is taught to mastery. Teaching to mastery ensures that students will be ready to move forward in the strand without the lessons becoming too difficult. Mastery communicates that what is learned today is important because it will be needed in later lessons.

A skill is considered mastered when every student is able to perform the skill independently without making any mistakes. The goal in each activity is to teach the skills to mastery before moving to the next activity. However, there may be a time when the students are having difficulty with a certain activity. In this instance, you may say, **Esto es muy difícil. Ahora vamos a continuar y luego volveremos a verlo. (This is really hard; let's go on and come back to this later.)** This should not occur often, but it is acceptable on rare occasions as long as you return to that activity before completing the lesson.

Determining Mastery

Mastery is assessed and determined mostly during the independent practice portion of the activities. Each student in the group must demonstrate the skill during independent practice with no errors. If a student makes an error, use the appropriate correction procedure, and practice the specific skill repeatedly until the student has mastered it. If a student needs any assistance, mastery has not been achieved.

Individual Practice

Provide every student an individual turn at the end of each activity. It is during individual practice that you determine whether each student has truly mastered the activity or if you need to provide additional group practice. As a rule, if more than two errors occur during individual practice, the group needs more practice.

Conducting Individual Practice

After group responses, call on each student individually to complete a few items or read a few sentences. Give each student one to three items during individual practice. You may need to give a stronger student only one item, but a weaker student may need two or three items to ensure mastery. Typically, you should call on lower-performing students first. Then you will call on a higher-performing student while encouraging the other students to answer in their heads. When all students can complete the task independently and without error, you know the group has achieved 100 percent mastery.

Lesson Mastery Sheet

At the end of each activity, tell students whether they have mastered the skill being taught. If they have, you will put a check mark on the Hoja de maestría (Mastery Sheet). This check indicates that every student in the group demonstrated mastery for the skill independently with no mistakes. If an error occurs during individual practice, provide additional instruction and group practice followed by another round of individual turns. Repeat this process until all students are able to perform the skill independently without error. At the end of each lesson, when all skills have been mastered, place a sticker (un adhesivo/una etiqueta) in the maestría column to indicate mastery of the entire lesson.

Hoja de maestría

Maestro/a _____   Grupo _____

Estudiantes _____

_____

_____

Actividad	1	2	3	4	5	6	7	8	9	10	Fluidez			Maestría
1														
2														
3														
4														
5														
6														
7														
8														
9														
10														

Lección

Make one copy for each group of students.

Placement and Assessment Guide, Spanish

8 Mastery Sheet

Staff Development Guide, Spanish

When Mastery Is Hard to Achieve

Occasionally it will be hard for the group to achieve mastery on a specific activity. If you sense that students are becoming frustrated, note the activity on the Hoja de maestría, and move to the next activity. You may need to leave the activity temporarily, but return to complete the activity later in the lesson or at the beginning of the next lesson.

Do *not* place a sticker on the Hoja de maestría for the lesson until mastery has been achieved. If students are still unable to achieve mastery, you may need to back up a lesson or two to review the activities that led up to the specific skill causing difficulty. If you have a specific student who is having difficulty achieving mastery on a skill, it is best to find a few extra minutes to work with that student individually.

Mastery Measurement

A series of student assessments is provided to assess student mastery of the skills presented in each of the **Teacher's Editions.** Students are assessed for mastery and generalization of letter-sound correspondences, word reading, and connected text. An assessment is administered every fifth lesson. The first eight assessments are timed for one minute. Starting with Assessment 9, students are also assessed for fluency. Those assessments (Assessments 9–24) are timed for one minute for parts 1, 2, 3 and one minute for part 4 (fluency).

Placing Students in SRA Intervenciones tempranas de la lectura

In order to appropriately place students in the *SRA Intervenciones tempranas de la lectura* program, administer a reliable and valid screening measure during the first several weeks of the school year. Many schools routinely give such tests to all students at the beginning of the year. If such tests are not routine at your school, initial teacher observations can be helpful in spotting students who should be screened to determine if they would benefit from *SRA Intervenciones tempranas de la lectura.*

One quick way to spot students in need of this intervention is to watch for students who are struggling to master the letter-sound, blending, and decoding instruction provided during the first several weeks of the school year. Students who consistently struggle with phonemic awareness activities during instruction may also need the extra help provided by the program. Of course, it becomes easier to notice students who are not making adequate progress as each week passes. However, it is important to identify students who need extra help as soon as possible because every day that passes allows students to fall farther and farther behind their peers. Our goal for all students is grade-level reading skills by the end of the year; the farther behind children fall at any point in the year, the more difficult it is for them to achieve that goal.

There are a number of tests currently available that can be used to screen students who need the support provided in *SRA Intervenciones tempranas de la lectura.*

Another method for determining placement is the use of a screening tool. In situations where no school-wide test is given, or if a student moves into your classroom after the school year has started, you may want to administer a screening test to help identify whether a student would benefit from the intervention instruction. Results of the screening test have the potential to help you identify students at risk of failing in reading earlier in the school year.

Placing students in the appropriate lessons is an essential part of ensuring student success in *SRA Intervenciones tempranas de la lectura.* Once a student has been identified as potentially benefiting from an early intervention curriculum, administer the Placement Test to students. The Placement Test, located on pages 3–6 of the **Placement and Assessment Guide,** consists of a series of short activities designed to mirror the content of the intervention materials at different points in the curriculum. Based on a student's demonstrated mastery of the skills in each of the Placement Test sections, you administer the next section of the test to the student, place the student in a specific lesson within the curriculum, or move the student out of the intervention group to receive instruction in only the primary reading materials.

Hora de brillar (Time to Shine)

Each week, you will send home with students the Hora de brillar certificado de lectura (Time to Shine Certificate). On this certificate, you will list the new letter names, letter-sound correspondences, vocabulary, and high-frequency words the student has mastered throughout the week. You will attach to the certificate a copy of the take-home version of the **Libros decodificables** the students have read during the week. The Hora de brillar certificado de lectura and the take-home version of the **Libros decodificables** help establish and maintain a connection between the teacher and each student's parents or guardian. A blackline master version of the Hora de brillar, in both Spanish and English, can be found in the back of the **Placement and Assessment Guide.**

Reflective Teaching

Even though *SRA Intervenciones tempranas de la lectura* is very structured, you will still need to reflect on your teaching to understand why your instruction is or is not having the desired effect with specific students. The purpose of this reflection is to gain awareness of your teaching practices and to formulate a plan of action to improve instruction as needed through critical decision-making. It may be helpful for you to keep a journal to document successes and challenges. (Journal entries should be made immediately after a lesson is finished and not during the actual lesson.) Over time, the journal entries will allow you to look for recurring patterns as you reflect on the needs of your students. It is also helpful to discuss both successes and challenges with colleagues, intervention coaches, or other educators.

The Phonology of Spanish

The Spanish language, unlike the English language, has a transparent writing system in which the correspondence between graphemes (written representations of sounds) and phonemes (the smallest units of sound) is predictable and apparent. The simple orthography of the Spanish language consists of five vowel sounds (*a, e, i, o, u*) that are well-defined and constant. In general, the phonetic structure of the Spanish language focuses on the syllable, a unit of pronunciation that has only one vowel sound. Syllables in Spanish consist of the open CV (consonant/vowel: ***pa pá***) pattern, the most frequent and common syllable type, and the CVC pattern (consonant/vowel/consonant: ***ven der***). Because of the consistency of letter-sound correspondences and the importance that vowels play within syllables, beginning Spanish reading instruction focuses on explicit syllabic instruction in which phonemes are manipulated (e.g., m*a,* m*e,* m*i,* m*o,* m*u*). In other words, beginning Spanish reading instruction (for example, phonemic awareness, word recognition and spelling) that attends to both syllables and phonemes is important.

There are thirty letters in the Spanish alphabet with twenty-seven letters and three consonant digraphs: *ll, ch,* and *rr.* These three digraphs are single consonants that are never separated. There is also one silent letter, *h* (example: *húmedo*), a letter that is used only in the spelling of foreign words, *w* (as in *Western* for a type of movie depicting the American West), and a letter, *x,* which when written is a blend of two phonemes. There are only two instances in which letters need to be together as a unit and pronounced as one sound: ***gu*** which is pronounced as /g/ and ***qu*** pronounced as /k/ (Signorini, 1997). Also, vowels that constitute a diphthong (two consecutive vowels that appear in one syllable: *ai/ay, ei/ey, oi/oy, au, eu, ou, ia , ie, io, ua, ue, uo*) or a triphthong (three consecutive vowels blended in one syllable: *iai, iei, iau, ioi, uai/uay, uei/uey, uau*) are not ever separated. Like English, the Spanish language also has consonant blends: *cr, pr, tr, br, gr, dr, fr, bl, cl, fl, pl, gl.*

In comparison to the English language, which has twenty-six letters in its alphabet and is composed of more than twenty-six speech sounds, the Spanish language is consistent with few irregularities. In comparison to English phonology, there are fewer sounds and letters to learn when beginning to read in Spanish. Students are quickly able to spell in Spanish.

Teaching and the Phonology of Spanish

Up to this point, the discussion of the phonology of Spanish has relied on some technical language, such as *phoneme, grapheme,* and *digraph.* However, when teaching children, such formal language is not used. Students do not need to know the theoretical concepts, but they are instead encouraged to develop automaticity in recognizing different letter-sound combinations. As you teach the **SRA Intervenciones tempranas de la lectura** curriculum, you will inevitably become increasingly familiar with the structure of Spanish, because the curriculum is carefully laid out to follow certain principles of Spanish phonology. To help you develop some of this background knowledge—or to refresh you on what you might have learned already—below is a review some of the major components and terms of the phonology of Spanish that are particularly useful when teaching **SRA Intervenciones tempranas de la lectura.**

Continuous and Stop Sounds

Continuous sounds are sounds that can be held, hummed, or sung. The most obvious continuous sounds are vowels; all vowel sounds *(a, e, i, o, u)* are continuous, including diphthongs (a blend of vowels in one syllable such as *oi* in *heroico*). Continuous consonants in Spanish include *f, l, j, m, n, ñ, r, rr, ll, s, v, w, x, y, z.* When you are teaching the **SRA Intervenciones tempranas de la lectura** curriculum, you will hold continuous sounds for two to three seconds. Holding continuous sounds makes sounding out and reading words fast easier for students.

Stop sounds are sounds that block the passage of air as the sound is completed. You cannot hold the /b/ sound for example, because the very act of making the sound stops the flow of air. The Spanish stop sounds are all consonants: *b, c, d, g, k, p, t, q.* Say the stop sounds quickly without distorting the sound. For example, the /b/ sound should not be distorted by the sound /uh/ at the end of it.

Syllable Types

A syllable is a unit of pronunciation that has one and only one vowel sound. There are two common syllable types in Spanish spelling: closed and open. Students are never taught the labels for each of these; however, the curriculum is written with a clear understanding of these syllable types so students are exposed to each of them.

Closed: A closed syllable ends in a consonant: *el, ven, pez, barcos*

Open: An open syllable ends in a vowel. Most syllables in Spanish are open and begin with a consonant: *sopa, ojo, bonito.*

Some terms that are familiar to you are avoided in this curriculum. Instead, students are taught to develop automaticity and to recognize the sounds they see, not the labels that go with the rules.

Spanish Syllable Patterns

The following syllable patterns occur in Spanish. Below, they are listed from the most common to the least frequently used syllable patterns:

1. CV
2. CVC
3. V
4. CCV
5. VC
6. CCVC
7. VCC
8. CVCC
9. CCVCC

Differences and Similarities in the Phonology of Spanish and English

Because most teachers who teach students to read in Spanish will eventually teach them to read in English, it is important to be aware of those elements that can cause confusion for students who will learn to read in both languages:

Basic Differences in Spanish and English Vowel Sounds:

- *a* in the Spanish word *casa* is similar to the English *o* in *octopus*
- *e* in the word *mesa* is similar to the English *e* in *red*
- *i* in the Spanish word *sin* is similar to the English sound in *seen*
- *o* in the Spanish word *dos* is similar to the Scotch-English sound in *auld*
- *u* in the Spanish word *uno* is similar to the English *oo* in *boot* or *fool.*

Note: There is no silent-e pattern in Spanish. In Spanish, the vowel **e** at the end of the word is pronounced as in the word *grande.*

English Phonics Elements That Do Not exist in Spanish Phonology:

- /w/ spelled **w** appears only in a small number of words borrowed from other languages
- Digraphs: **sh, th, wh, ph, gh, -ng**
- **S-blends**
- Final consonant blends (e.g., *switch*)
- /**k**/ spelled **k.** In Spanish, the letter **k** appears only in a small number of words borrowed from other languages.

The Sound Pronunciation Guide on the following pages corresponds to the sounds and spellings taught in **SRA Intervenciones tempranas de la lectura.**

Sound Pronunciation Guide

a	año, pata	father	
b	boca, embargo	bib	Initial in the word or with *m,* similar to English *b*
	labio, tabla		Between vowels or before *l* or *r,* more like the *v* in *lever*
c	cedro, civil	cedar	*c* before *e* or *i*: in most of Spain, similar to the *th* in *thick;* in southern Spain and Latin America, similar to the English *s*
	cable, cobre	cat	The hard *c* in Spanish is not aspirated as it is in English
ch*	chiste, muchacho	church	*No longer alphabetized as a separate letter
d	dar, falda	deed	Initial in the word or after *n* or *l,* similar to English *d,* but not aspirated
	lodo, padre		In all other positions, similar to the *th* in *rather*
e	denso, espada	pet	When the syllable ends in a consonant, similar to the *e* in *pet*
	me, pero	café	When the syllable ends in a vowel, similar to the *e* in *café*
f	fuerte, sofá	fat	
g	general, gitano		Before *e* or *i,* similar to the strongly aspirated *h* in *ha!*
	gato, grupo		The hard *g* is not aspirated as it is in English
h	honor, ahora		Is always silent
i	silla, grito	machine	
j	jugo, pájaro		Similar to the strongly aspirated *h* in *ha!*
k	kilo, kimono	kick	Not aspirated as it is in English
l	listo, oler	lid	
ll*	llamar, olla		In most of Spain, similar to the *lli* in *million;* in southern Spain and most of Spanish America, similar to the *j* in *jar;* in Argentina and Uruguay, similar to the *s* in *vision;* *no longer alphabetized as a separate letter
m	masa, amargo	mum	
n	sin, nota, tono	no	

Sound Pronunciation Guide

	rencor, fango		Before hard *c* or *g*, sounds like the *ng* of *thing*
ñ	riña		Sounds like the *ny* in *canyon*
o	sordo, toldo	cord	When the syllable ends in a consonant, sounds like the *o* in *cord*
	lodo, ocupar	note	When the syllable ends in a vowel, sounds like the *o* in *note*
p	parte, capa	pot	Not aspirated as it is in English
q	quinto, níquel	pique	Pronounced like an unaspirated *k*
r	raya, enredo		Initial in the word or after *l, n,* or *s,* it is strongly trilled
	caro, contar		Elsewhere, pronounced with a flap of the tongue like the *dd* in *ladder*
rr*	carro		Is strongly trilled; *not alphabetized as a separate letter
s	cosa, sino	salty	
t	tonto, matar	tight	Not aspirated as it is in English
u	luto, útil	rude	
	quince, guerra		Silent when preceded by *q* or in *gui* and *gue,* unless marked by dieresis
	agüero, güiro		When marked by dieresis, sounds like the *u* in *Guinevere*
v	vino, vista		Initial in the word, sounds like the *b* in *bib*
	lavar, salvo		In all other positions it is softer, more like the *v* in *level*
w	wat, water		Pronounced like either the English *v* or *w*
x	éxito, exacto		Pronounced like either the *x* of *exit* or the *gs* of *eggs*
	mixta, experto		Sometimes softened to the sound of an *s*
	México		In the words *México* and *mexicano,* sounds like the aspirated *h* in *ha!*
y	yeso, suyo	young	Initial in the word or between vowels, is like the *y* in *young;* in Argentina and Uruguay sounds like the *s* in *vision* between vowels

The Strands

This section explains each of the strands and how to carry out the activities that support each strand. Sample activities are provided for easy reference.

Strand One: Phonemic Awareness

In the Phonemic Awareness Strand, students listen to and manipulate sounds within words, which lays the foundation for learning letter-sound correspondences and for word-recognition skills. In this strand, students learn to segment words into individual sounds or syllables and to blend the sounds or syllables back into words before sounding out whole words. Later, students will listen for each sound they hear in a word and spell each sound in the order they hear it.

For the activities illustrated in this section, you will notice that students are never asked to look at words or to map sounds to visual symbols. Instead, students develop auditory sensitivity to the sounds they will later learn to match to written letters when decoding words. This auditory sensitivity, which helps students notice and distinguish sounds in speech, will greatly benefit them in later lessons as they begin to map the sounds they hear to written alphabetic symbols.

Phonemic Awareness is carefully sequenced to facilitate learning. Students move from easier to harder skills as they progress across lessons. Initial sound recognition is taught first because this is the easiest sound for students to distinguish in a word, followed by last sounds, and then medial sounds. Students then progress through Auditory Blending, Segmenting, and Stretching and Blending, as one skill builds upon the last.

Phonemic Awareness (Teacher's Edition A)

Several activities are typical in the Phonemic Awareness Strand in the first part of the school year. The activities introduced in **Teacher's Edition A** come from two categories of phonemic awareness skills, Sound Discrimination and Segmentation and Blending, which are discussed more fully below in the order they are introduced in the curriculum.

FORMATS

- Sound Discrimination

   First-Sound Game
   Ending-Sound Game
   Sound Position: Thumbs Up—Thumbs Down

- Segmentation and Blending

   Oral Blending
   Stretching Words
   Stretch and Blend

All of the phonemic awareness activities in **Teacher's Edition A** have one thing in common. They all include a special "modeling" phase, in which you introduce students to the new activities. At the beginning stage, you are teaching students not just the concepts (in this case the concepts involved in developing phonemic awareness) but also your techniques for working with them on learning the new concepts. For example, in the first phonemic awareness activity described below, First-Sound Game, you model for your students both how to identify the first sounds of words and how to play the game itself. Over time, your students will learn how to play the game, so this modeling strategy will be phased out.

After the activity has been adequately modeled, your students will no longer need the model, so you will be using a basic activity structure. This basic activity structure appears in this guide as a series of steps labeled "Activity at a Glance."

Phonemic Awareness (Teacher's Edition A): Sound Discrimination

There are three basic sound discrimination formats, First-Sound Game, Ending-Sound Game, and Sound Position. In these activities, students learn to distinguish between sounds within words and to identify sound position within words (beginning, ending, or middle). There are two variations of sound position: "beginning or ending" and "thumbs up—thumbs down."

First-Sound Game

Because the beginning sounds of words are the easiest for students to distinguish, students listen for those from the very first day of the intervention. This also allows students to connect initial sounds of key words later when learning letter-sound correspondences.

The format for teaching the First-Sound Game is very straightforward. Say a word emphasizing the first sound in that word. Say the word so students hear the first sound distinctly. Ask your students, **¿Cuál es el primer sonido? (What is the first sound?)** Cue the students to answer together by quickly holding up your index finger. It is important that you do not mouth sounds with students when it is their turn to answer. Repeat the procedure with the remaining words.

ACTIVITY AT A GLANCE

- Step 1: Tell your students that they are going to be listening for a sound at the beginning, at the ending, or in the middle of a word. You will be working with only one sound position at a time within the word.

- Step 2: Say a word, emphasizing the sound you want your students to hear in such a way that the students can hear that sound distinctly from the rest of the word, for example, /aaa/ma. **(What is the first sound in /aaa/ma?)**

- Step 3: Ask your students to tell you what sound they hear in the specified position within a word: **¿Cuál es el primer sonido que escuchan en /aaa/ma?**

- Step 4: Give your students a second or two of think time, and then cue them to respond in unison by holding up your index finger. Do not say the sound with them.

- Step 5: Repeat the procedure with the remaining words. **Siguiente palabra, /mmm/osca. ¿Cuál es el primer sonido que escuchan en /mmm/osca? (Next word, /mmm/osca. What is the first sound in /mmm/osca?)** Cue the students to answer. Correct all errors as they occur.

- Step 6: End with individual mastery check by giving each student one or two words.

Sometimes students give the letter's *name* instead of the *sound* for the answer. They say *eme* instead of /*mmm*/. Model how to say the *sound* and not the letter's *name*. Have students practice saying the sound.

Students catch on to this game rather quickly. The first sounds are usually easy for them, but the ending and middle sounds are often more difficult. If students are unable to identify a sound, correct by stretching the word. For example, sometimes they will listen for the last sound in a word: **Escuchen.**

/mmm/eee/sss/aaa/. (Listen, /mmm/eee/sss/aaa/.) Tap on the finger that is raised for the last sound in the word and ask again, **¿Cuál es el último sonido que escuchan en /mmm/eee/sss/aaa/? (What is the last sound that you hear in /mmm/eee/sss/aaa?)** Because students are having trouble identifying the correct sound, you may need to emphasize the sound by holding it a little longer than usual.

When in doubt, correct with the Model-Lead-Test strategy.

Questions and Answers

Lesson 3

Activity 4
Sound Discrimination
Part A: First-Sound Game

Note: Emphasize the beginning sound in the word when you say it to students. Hold continuous sounds for a full 2 seconds so students can hear the beginning sound distinctly from the rest of the word.

Vamos a hacer algo diferente. Ahora vamos a prestar atención al sonido que oímos al principio de una palabra. Voy a decir una palabra. Escuchen el primer sonido de la palabra y díganlo cuando dé la señal. Ésta es la señal que utilizaré. *(Hold up one finger).*

Mi turno. La palabra es *ama*. *(Pause.)* /Aaa/ma. *(Pause.)* **¿Cuál es el primer sonido que escucho en *ama*?** /Aaa/. **Háganlo conmigo. Escuchen.** *Ama*. *(Pause.)* /Aaa/ma. *(Pause.)* **¿Cuál es el primer sonido que escuchamos?**

(Teacher and students:) /aaa/

Ahora, ustedes solos. Siguiente palabra. *Mosca*. *(Pause.)* /Mmm/osca. **¿Cuál es el primer sonido que escuchan en *mosca*?** *(Cue students by holding up one finger.)* /mmm/

(Scaffold as necessary. Use the model-lead-test strategy when a student makes a mistake.)

ERROR CORRECTION:
Mi turno. *(Say the sound of the initial letter of the word for 2 seconds.)* **El primer sonido en la palabra /mmm/osca es /mmm/.**
(Ask all students to repeat the sound.)
Ahora, ustedes juntos. /mmm/
Ahora vamos a hacerlo otra vez. *(Back up 2 items and restart the activity.)*

Siguiente palabra.

Repeat the process with the following words: amigo, araña, mercado.

¡Buen trabajo diciendo el primer sonido que escuchan en las palabras!

Individual Practice

(Provide individual practice with 2 or 3 words per student.)

¡Buen trabajo diciendo el primer sonido que escuchan en las palabras!

---

23 Lesson 3

Part B: Ending Sound

Note: When saying the word, hold up one finger for each sound in the word. Emphasize the end sound. Students will associate the last finger with the end sound. Hold continuous sounds for a full 2 seconds so students can hear the end sound distinctly from the rest of the word.

Ahora, vamos a prestar atención al último sonido que oímos de la palabra. Esto es un poco más difícil. Yo lo haré primero.

Mi turno. Escuchen. *Ama.* *(Pause.)* **/Aaa/mmm/aaa/.** *(When saying the word, hold up one finger for each sound in the word.)*

¿Cuál es el último sonido que escucho en *ama?* *(Cue students by wiggling the finger that corresponds with the end sound in the word. In ama, draw attention to the third finger.)* **/Aaa/.**

Mi turno nuevamente. Escuchen. *Sol.* *(Pause.)* **/Sss/ooo/lll/.** *(Hold up one finger for each sound in the word.)* **¿Cuál es el último sonido que escucho en *sol?*** *(Wiggle the finger that corresponds with the end sound.)* **/Lll/.**

(Scaffold as necessary.)

Háganlo conmigo. *Me.* *(Pause.)* **/Mmm/eee/.** *(Hold up one finger for each sound in the word.)* **¿Cuál es el último sonido que escuchamos en *me?*** *(Wiggle the finger that corresponds with the end sound.)* (Teacher and students:) **/eee/**

Siguiente. *Mes.* *(Pause.)* **/Mmm/eee/sss/.**

(Hold up one finger for each sound in the word.) **¿Cuál es el último sonido que escuchamos en *mes?*** *(Wiggle the finger that corresponds with the end sound: /sss/.)* (Teacher and students:) **/sss/**

Ustedes solos. *Mira.* *(Pause.)* **/Mmm/iii/rrr/aaa/.** *(Hold up one finger for each sound in the word.)* **¿Cuál es el último sonido que escuchan en *mira?*** *(Wiggle the finger that corresponds with the end sound.)* **/aaa/**

(Monitor, and correct. Scaffold as necessary.)

Siguiente. *Es.* *(Pause.)* **/Eee/sss/.** *(Hold up one finger for each sound in the word.)* **¿Cuál es el último sonido que escuchan en *es?*** *(Wiggle the finger that corresponds with the end sound.)* **/sss/**

¡Buen trabajo diciendo el último sonido que escuchan en las palabras!

Individual Practice

(Provide individual practice with 2 or 3 words per student.)

¡Buen trabajo diciendo el último sonido que escuchan en las palabras!

Terminamos esta actividad. ¡Buen trabajo diciendo el primer y el último sonido que escuchan en las palabras! Ahora puedo marcar la caja para esta actividad en la Hoja de maestría.

Sound Position: Thumbs Up—Thumbs Down

In this activity, students listen to words and say whether the words begin or end with a specific sound. If a word starts with the target sound, students hold their thumbs in an up position. If the word does not start with the target sound, students hold their thumbs in a down position.

- Step 1: Tell your students they are going to play a game to help them listen for a sound at the beginning of a word.

- Step 2: Remind students of the rules of the game. If they hear the sound at the beginning of the word, they will put their thumbs up. If they do not hear the sound at the beginning of the word, they will put their thumbs down.

- Step 3: As you say the word, emphasize the sound you want your students to identify, so that they can hear that sound distinctly from the rest of the word: **/aaa/lto.**

- Step 4: Repeat the word, emphasizing the sound, and cue students to put their thumbs up or down according to whether they hear the sound at the beginning of the word.

- Step 5: Repeat the procedure with the remaining words. Remember to correct all errors as soon as they occur.

- Step 6: End with individual mastery check by giving each student one or two words.

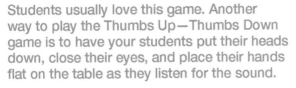

IN THE REAL WORLD

Students usually love this game. Another way to play the Thumbs Up—Thumbs Down game is to have your students put their heads down, close their eyes, and place their hands flat on the table as they listen for the sound.

Correct errors with Model-Test error correction technique.

Questions and Answers . . . .

Activity 2
Thumbs Up–Thumbs Down Game

En esta actividad vamos a jugar a "¿Pulgares arriba o abajo?". ¿Recuerdan este juego?

Voy a decir una palabra y quiero que escuchen si comienza con el sonido /aaa/. (*Hold up the **Aa** Tarjeta de sonido. Touch under a.*) ¿Cuál sonido van a escuchar? (*Touch under a.*) /aaa/

Correcto. Si la palabra comienza con el sonido /aaa/, apunten su pulgar hacia arriba. (*Demonstrate a thumbs-up.*) Si no escuchan el sonido /aaa/ al principio de la palabra, entonces apunten su pulgar hacia abajo. (*Demonstrate a thumbs-down.*)

Preparen su pulgar. Escuchen atentamente a ver si las palabras que voy a decir comienzan con el sonido /aaa/. (*Touch under a.*) ¿Cuál es el sonido que van a escuchar? (*Touch under a.*) /aaa/

¿Qué van a hacer cuando escuchen el sonido /aaa/ al principio de la palabra? (*Students should give a thumbs-up.*)

¿Qué van a hacer si no escuchan el sonido /aaa/ al principio de la palabra? (*Students should give a thumbs-down.*)

¡Muy bien!

Mi turno. /Aaa/banico.
¿Escucho /aaa/ al principio de abanico? Sí, así que apunto mi pulgar hacia arriba. (*Demonstrate a thumbs-up.*)

Háganlo conmigo. Listos. /Aaa/lto.
¿Escuchamos /aaa/ al principio de /aaa/lto? (*Teacher and students should give a thumbs-up.*)

¡Muy bien! **Alto** comienza con el sonido /aaa/.

Ahora todos bajen sus manos.
Siguiente palabra. (*Pause.*) /Ooo/so.
¿Escuchan /aaa/ al principio de /ooo/so? (*Students should give a thumbs-down.*)

(*Scaffold as necessary. Emphasize the beginning /aaa/ sound in each word. If a student makes a mistake, immediately stop and use the model-lead-test strategy.*)

ERROR CORRECTION:
Mi turno. Escuchen nuevamente.
(*Repeat the word.*)
La palabra es /ooo/so. No escucho /aaa/ al principio de la palabra oso, así que apunto mi pulgar hacia abajo. (*Demonstrate holding your thumb down.*)
Ahora, ustedes juntos. ¿Escuchan /aaa/ al principio de la palabra oso? No. ¿Entonces, qué hacen? (*Check to make sure that all thumbs are down.*)
Ahora vamos a hacerlo otra vez. (*Back up 2 items and restart the activity.*)

Siguiente palabra.

Repeat the process with the following words: Ana, ángel, banco, Lola, alambre.

¡Buen trabajo reconociendo las palabras que comienzan con /aaa/ y las palabras que no comienzan con /aaa/!

Individual Practice
(*Provide individual practice.*)

¡Buen trabajo reconociendo las palabras que comienzan con /aaa/!

Completaron esta actividad perfectamente. Ahora puedo marcar la caja para esta actividad en la Hoja de maestría.

Phonemic Awareness (Teacher's Edition A): Segmentation and Blending

There are three formats focusing on phonemic segmentation and blending: Oral Blending, Segmenting, and Stretch and Blend. Blending is combining sounds in order to make a syllable or a whole word. Segmentation is the separation of a word into its individual sounds or syllables. Practicing segmenting further promotes auditory sensitivity to individual phonemes in words. Segmentation is explained to students as stretching words. Stretching is a more difficult skill for students than oral blending, so oral blending is taught first.

Oral Blending

A puppet named Pepe is introduced into the curriculum when the students begin to blend words orally. Pepe says words phoneme by phoneme or syllable by syllable. In other words, Pepe stretches out words instead of saying them normally. Students are told they are helping Pepe learn to speak normally. When teaching oral blending, move Pepe's mouth as though he is the one talking. Students should watch Pepe closely as he speaks.

In the oral-blending activities, say the words very slowly, emphasizing the individual sounds or syllables in multisyllabic words. The students say the words at a normal rate.

ACTIVITY AT A GLANCE

- Step 1: Introduce Pepe to your students. Tell them he says words in a "funny" way. Ask your students to help you teach Pepe to speak better by saying the fast way the words he says funny (or stretches).
- Step 2: Demonstrate how Pepe talks by moving his mouth as you say a word slowly: **/Aaa/mmm/aaa/.**

- Step 3: Ask your students, **¿Qué palabra estiró Pepe? (What word did Pepe stretch?)** On your cue, the students answer in unison, **ama.**
- Step 4: Repeat the procedure with the remaining words. Remember to correct all errors as they occur.
- Step 5: End with individual mastery check by having each student blend two or three words.

IN THE REAL WORLD

- Sometimes students leave off a sound or invert sounds when they blend the sounds back into a whole word. Together with Pepe, you can model the correct blending of the word. Pepe then repeats the word in his stretched-out way, and the students get another chance to blend the word correctly.

- Developing a personality for Pepe as he interacts with the students can be a motivational tool for keeping the students engaged in the lesson.

Questions and Answers

Activity 9
Oral Blending
Say the Word Game

(Use Pepe the puppet to speak words in stretched form.)

Vamos a jugar a un juego nuevo. Se llama "¡Digan la palabra!". Así es como jugamos "¡Digan la palabra!". Éste es nuestro amigo Pepe. Pepe no puede decir las palabras como nosotros. A él le gusta estirar las palabras lentamente. Cuando Pepe hable, ustedes tienen que escuchar atentamente y decirme qué palabra estiró Pepe.

Voy a decirle una palabra a Pepe y él la estirará. Cuando lo indique, digan la palabra que oyeron.

(Pretend to whisper the word ama to Pepe.)

(Pepe:) **/Aaa/mmm/aaa/.**

(Pause.) **¿Qué palabra estiró Pepe?** *(Cue students using the hand-drop cue.)* **ama**

¡Muy bien! Él dijo ama.

Siguiente palabra. Escuchen.

(Move Pepe's mouth as if he were stretching the word. Pepe:) **/Sss/ooo/lll/.**

¿Qué palabra estiró Pepe? *(Cue students using the hand-drop cue.)* **sol**

¡Buen trabajo diciendo la palabra que estiró Pepe!

Listos. Siguiente palabra.

Repeat the process with the following words: en, sal, va.

(Scaffold as necessary.)

Individual Practice

(Provide individual practice with 1 word per student.)

Terminamos esta actividad. Vamos a marcar la Hoja de maestría. Contemos las marcas todos juntos. Al final, indicaremos que hemos terminado la lección.

¡Buen trabajo! Han completado todas las actividades de esta lección y ahora tienen las habilidades que se enseñaron en cada actividad. Ahora Pepe quiere darles un abrazo.

Ya que hemos terminado todas las partes de nuestra lección, puedo poner un adhesivo en la Hoja de maestría de esta lección.

Lesson 4

Activity 7
Oral Blending
Multisyllabic Words

Note: You may want to use the hand-drop cue in this activity. (Hand up to your shoulder, palm of hand facing students. Ask the question, pause, and then quickly lower your hand, palm down.)

(Put on Pepe the puppet.)

Pepe no puede hablar como nosotros. Le gusta hablar lentamente. Necesitamos ayudarlo a decir rápidamente las palabras. Cuando Pepe hable, ustedes tienen que escuchar bien y decirme qué dijo.

(Pretend to whisper a word to Pepe.)

Yo ayudaré a Pepe. Escuchen. *(Move Pepe's mouth as if he is saying each syllable in the word salsa. Pepe:) Sal/sa. (Pause.)* **¿Qué palabra dijo Pepe? Salsa.**

(Pretend to whisper a word to Pepe.)

Ahora, ustedes solos. Escuchen. *(Move Pepe's mouth as if he is saying each syllable. Pepe:) Fue/go. (Pause.) (Pepe:) Fue/go.* **¿Qué palabra dijo Pepe?** *(Pause. Hand-drop cue.)* **fuego**

¡Muy bien! Él dijo fuego.

(Scaffold as necessary.)

Listos. *(Pause.)* **Siguiente palabra.**

> **Repeat the process with the following words: li/bro, pla/ya, ma/má, can/sa/da, la/na, a/ma, pa/pá, plu/ma.**

(Scaffold as necessary.)

Individual Practice

(Provide individual practice.)

¡Buen trabajo! Hemos terminado todas las partes de nuestra lección. ¿Saben lo que significa eso? ¡Significa que puedo poner un adhesivo en la Hoja de maestría de esta lección!

Stretching Words

Stretching a word takes place only in the first few lessons. Segmenting is explained to students as "stretching" a word. A word is stretched so that each sound in the word can be heard. When stretching words, students stretch out each sound and do not stop between sounds. Students should sound like they are humming the words. Continuous sounds are held two to three seconds. Stop sounds are said quickly.

For this format, you will say a word. Students then say the sounds in the word, holding up one finger for each sound. When students hold up a finger for each sound in a word, it creates a multi-sensory component that helps them to distinguish between sounds. You will guide the process by holding up a finger for each sound without saying the sounds yourself.

ACTIVITY AT A GLANCE

- Step 1: Tell your students they are going to stretch words. Remind them that they need to hold up one finger for each sound they hear in the word as they stretch it.

- Step 2: Say the word. **Me.** *(Pause.)* **Estiren** *me.* **(Stretch the word** *me.***)**

- Step 3: Cue students to begin stretching by holding up your index finger. Students say the word sound by sound, holding up one finger for each sound. Guide the process by holding up a finger for each sound without saying the sounds yourself.

- Step 4: Repeat the procedure with the remaining words. Correct all errors as they occur.

- Step 5: End with individual mastery check by having each student stretch one or two words.

IN THE REAL WORLD

Create a left-to-right orientation from the *student's* perspective for this activity. Use your right fist with the back of your hand facing your students. Raise your index finger for the first sound, then your middle finger, ring finger, and so on. This directionality helps students learn the left-to-right orientation necessary for reading text.

Questions and Answers

An error students may make is adding the short /u/ sound to the end of stop sounds. For example, the word *mapa* should be stretched */mmm/aaa/p/aaa/* and not */mmm/aaa/puh/aaa/*. By noticing this early, you can help your students make the sound correctly by modeling the correct pronunciation of the sound. Then have the students repeat the sound.

Lesson 1

Activity 6
Stretch the Word Game

Note: Remember to hold each continuous sound for about 2 seconds.

Éste es un juego nuevo. Se llama "¡Estirando palabras!". Así es como jugamos "¡Estirando palabras!". Diré una palabra, y me dirán los sonidos que oyen en la palabra o estirarán la palabra. Vamos a aprender cómo estirar palabras. Observen cómo lo hago. Primero levanto mi mano con el puño cerrado. *(Demonstrate.)* **Luego, levanto un dedo por cada sonido de la palabra que estoy diciendo.**

La primera palabra es mi. *(Pause.)* **/Mmm/iii/.** *(Demonstrate by raising 1 finger for each sound in mi as you say the sound.)* **¿Ven cómo levanto un dedo por cada sonido que estiro en la palabra mi?**

Háganlo conmigo. Levanten su puño. Estiremos mi. *(Hold up one finger for each sound with students.)* */mmm/iii/*

(Teacher and students:) /mmm/iii/

(Scaffold as necessary.)

ERROR CORRECTION:

(Remind students the sound of the letter m is /mmm/.)

Recuerden que el sonido de la letra m es /mmm/. ¿Cuál es el sonido de la letra m? /mmm/

¡Muy bien! M es la primera letra de /mmm/i y el sonido de m es /mmm/. Ahora, escuchen el siguiente sonido en mi. *(Pause.)* **/iii/. La palabra mi tiene dos sonidos, /mmm/ e /iii/. /Mmm/iii/.** *(Hold up one finger for each sound.)*

Si estamos levantando nuestros dedos cuando decimos cada sonido de la palabra, ¿qué hacen cuando estiran la palabra mi? *(Check each student. Be sure they are correctly holding up one finger for each sound in the word.)* **¡Muy bien!**

Siguiente palabra. Me. Estiren me. */Mmm/eee/.* *(Pause. Demonstrate by raising one finger for each sound in me.) /mmm/eee/*

(Scaffold as necessary.)

(Repeat until all students can stretch me. If a student makes a mistake, immediately stop and use the model-lead-test strategy.)

ERROR CORRECTION:

Mi turno. Escuchen y miren nuevamente. /Mmm/eee/. *(Pause. Demonstrate by raising one finger for each sound in me.)*

Ahora, háganlo conmigo. /Mmm/eee/. *(Teacher and students should hold up one finger for each sound as the word is stretched.)* **¡Muy bien!**

Ahora, ustedes juntos. */mmm/eee/* *(Check each student. Be sure they are correctly holding up one finger for each sound in the word.)*

Ahora vamos a hacerlo otra vez. *(Back up 2 items and restart the activity.)*

Individual Practice

(Provide individual practice.)

¡Buen trabajo! Terminamos esta actividad correctamente. Puedo marcar esta caja en la Hoja de maestría y podemos pasar a la siguiente actividad.

---

8 Lesson 1

Stretch and Blend

After learning the separate skills of oral blending and stretching, your students will be required to combine the two skills into Stretch and Blend. These activities prepare students for sounding out written words and then blending them back together in order to read them.

Pepe the puppet is still a motivational tool. During stretch and blend activities, Pepe is placed on the table. The students are told that Pepe is still learning to speak normally, the fast way. Eventually Pepe "graduates." He has learned to speak the fast way, and he says goodbye to the students.

ACTIVITY AT A GLANCE

- Step 1: Place Pepe on the table.
- Step 2: Have students hold up their fists. Demonstrate by holding up your fist also.
- Step 3: Tell student to stretch the word. *Masa.* **Estiren** *masa.* **(Stretch** *masa.***)**
- Step 4: Cue students to begin stretching. Hold up one finger for each sound to guide the students. Do not say the sounds with the students.
- Step 5: Students say the word, one sound at a time, holding up one finger for each sound.

- Step 6: Ask the students, **¿Qué palabra estiraron? (What word did you stretch?)** Cue students to answer.
- Step 7: Repeat the procedure with the remaining words. Correct all errors.
- Step 8: End with individual mastery check by having students stretch and blend one or two words.

IN THE REAL WORLD

It is important to give immediate corrective feedback to your students when they make an error. All errors should be corrected as soon as they occur. There are several types of errors that can be made by students during stretch and/or blend activities:

- Saying the word slowly instead of fast.
- Saying the word fast instead of stretching it.
- Leaving out a sound (Teacher says /sss/aaa/lll/; students say /sss/aaa/).

- Saying a different sound (Teacher says /sss/aaa/lll/; students say /sss/ooo/lll/.
- Adding an extra sound (Teacher says /aaa/lll/aaa/; students say /aaa/lll/aaa/sss/).
- Saying a word and accentuating a different syllable (Teacher says /p/aaa/p/**aaa/** Papá; students say /p/aaa/p/aaa/ papa.

Use the error correction technique, Model-Lead-Test, to correct Stretch and Blend errors.

Questions and Answers

Lesson 12

Activity 4
Stretch and Blend

(Place Pepe on the table.)

Van a continuar enseñando a Pepe cómo hablar correctamente. Recuerden que Pepe siempre estira cada palabra que dice. Ustedes van a estirar palabras como lo hace Pepe y después van a decirlas rápidamente. Observen cómo lo hago.

Mamá. *(Raise your fist and hold up 1 finger for each sound as you stretch the word.)* **/Mmm/aaa/mmm/aaa/.**

Ahora ustedes. Puños arriba. *(Demonstrate.)* **Estiren *mamá*.**

La palabra es *mamá*. *(Demonstrate by raising your fist and holding up 1 finger for each sound, but do not say the sounds with students.)* **/mmm/aaa/mmm/aaa/**
¿Qué palabra estiraron? mamá
Díganla rápidamente. mamá

(Scaffold as necessary.)

(Check students for correct use of hand cues while stretching the word. Also mention the accent marks.) **Recuerden que el acento nos ayuda a pronunciar las palabras correctamente. El acento enfatiza el sonido de una letra en la palabra. Cuando una palabra tiene acento, el sonido de la letra acentuada se pronuncia con más énfasis. El acento en la palabra nos ayuda a pronunciarla correctamente y distinguir su significado.** *(Emphasize the different pronunciations of papa and papá.)* **Por ejemplo, papa y papá no significan la misma cosa.**

Siguiente palabra. *(Pause.)* ***Papá.***

Estiren *papá*. *(Hold up 1 finger for each sound, but do not say the sounds.)* **/p/aaa/p/aaa/**
¿Qué palabra estiraron? papá
Díganla rápidamente. papá

> Repeat the process with the following words: **sala, sopa, loma, sapo.**

Individual Practice

(Provide individual practice with 2 words per student.)

¡Buen trabajo estirando y formando palabras! Terminamos esta actividad correctamente. Puedo marcar esta caja en la Hoja de maestría y podemos pasar a la siguiente actividad.

97 Lesson 12

Phonemic Awareness (Teacher's Edition A) Phonological Awareness

SRA Intervenciones tempranas de la lectura includes instructional tasks that focus on the syllabic nature of learning to read in Spanish. These auditory activities help students listen to sounds and build syllables and join syllables to form multisyllabic words.

These activities appear in **Teacher's Edition A** and later become incorporated in written tasks in the Word Recognition and Spelling Strand in **Teacher's Edition B,** preparing students to read syllables in isolation, chunk words into syllables to read the word, and write multisyllabic words. It is important that students master these skills, because the skills prepare students for future complex reading and writing/spelling tasks.

To ensure that students learn the procedure for these auditory tasks and master the skills, it is important to use the Model-Lead-Test technique in the initial lessons.

Listening to Syllables

In this activity, students learn to segment words into syllables. After Lesson 1, Activity 7, Pepe the puppet teaches students how to segment words into syllables.

Model the procedure by using Pepe to say the word fast: **Gato.** Say and clap for each syllable in the word: *ga (clap)* **to** *(clap).* Then say, **¿Qué palabra dijo? (What word did he say?)** *(Pause.)* **Gato.** Students listen as you say the word again. **Gato.** Say and clap for each syllable in the word together with the students: *ga (clap)* **to** *(clap).* Then, students listen to Pepe as he says the word again: *(Pause.)* **Gato.** Students say and clap for each syllable in the word: *ga (clap) to (clap).*

Then say, **¿Qué palabra dijo? (What word did he say?)** *(Pause.)* **Gato.** Repeat the process with the remaining words and provide individual practice for each student to segment the syllables in 2–3 words.

Activity 5
Phonological Awareness

Listening to Syllables

(Put on Pepe the puppet.)

Note: Use the following process in this activity:
1. Say the word first.
2. Ask students to break the word into syllables by clapping for each part (dar una palmada). **Separen esta palabra en sílabas y den una palmada por cada sílaba.**
3. Have the students say the word fast. **Digan la palabra rápidamente.**

Pepe ha regresado. Pepe ahora nos va a enseñar cómo dar una palmada por cada sílaba de la palabra.

Pepe dirá una palabra y todos vamos a dar una palmada por cada sílaba de la palabra.

Mi turno.

(Pepe:) **Gato.** *(Pause.)*
Ga *(clap)* **to** *(clap). (Model clapping for each syllable.)* **¿Qué palabra dijo? Gato.**

ERROR CORRECTION:
If students do not agree on the number of syllables or clap the wrong number of times according to the syllables of the word, say **Vamos a dar palmadas nuevamente. Escuchen.** Say the word in syllables, and clap according to the number of syllables.

Háganlo conmigo. Escuchen. *(Pause.)*
(Pepe:) **Gato.**
(Pepe and students:) **ga** *(clap)* **to** *(clap)*

¿Cuál es la palabra?
(Teacher and students:) **gato**

Ahora, ustedes solos.
Listos. Escuchen.

(Pepe:) **Gato.** *(cue.)* **ga** *(clap)* **to** *(clap)*
¿Qué palabra? gato
(Scaffold as necessary.)

Siguiente palabra.

Escuchen. *(Pause.)*

(Pepe:) **Mi.**
(Cue.) **mi** *(clap)*
¿Qué palabra? mi
Siguiente palabra.

Repeat the process with the following words: ra/ta, el, pa/la, se, ma/la, tú, so/lo.

Individual Practice

(Provide individual practice.)

Han hecho un gran trabajo, ¿y saben lo que significa eso? Marcaré esta actividad en la Hoja de maestría, y pasaremos a nuestra siguiente actividad.

Building Syllables

In this activity, students learn that a syllable is part of a word and that syllables are formed by joining sounds together.

Touch under the letter on the *Tarjeta de sonido* and say, **¿Cuál es el sonido de esta letra? /mmm/. (What is this letter's sound?)** Next, model how to form a syllable: **Si digo /mmm/ y /aaa/ juntos forman *ma*. (If I say /mmm/ and then /aaa/ they form the syllable *ma*.)** Students now form a syllable with you: **Háganlo conmigo.**

Digo /mmm/ y añado /eee/. ¿Qué sílaba se forma? (Let's do it together. I say /mmm/ and then I say /eee/. What syllable do they form together?) *(Pause.)* ***me*.** Have students demonstrate their ability to form a syllable. Say, **Ustedes solos. Digo /mmm/ y añado /ooo/. (Your turn. I say /mmm/ and then I say /ooo/.)** *(Pause.)* **¿Qué sílaba se forma? (What syllable do they form together?)** *mo*. Repeat the process to form the remaining syllables and provide individual practice for each student to segment 2–3 words into syllables.

Lesson 4

Activity 3
Phonological Awareness
Building Syllables

Ahora vamos a formar sílabas. Recuerden que una sílaba es parte de una palabra, y podemos formar una sílaba cuando juntamos sonidos.

(Hold up the Mm Tarjeta de sonido.) ¿Cuál es el sonido de esta letra? *(Touch under m.)* *(Call on individual students.)* /mmm/

Mi turno. Escuchen. Si digo /mmm/ y añado /aaa/, se forma la sílaba ma. /Mmm/ y /aaa/ juntos forman ma.

Háganlo conmigo. Digo /mmm/ y añado /eee/.
¿Qué sílaba se forma? *(Pause.)* *(Teacher and students:)* me

Háganlo conmigo. Digo /mmm/ y añado /iii/.
¿Qué sílaba se forma? *(Pause.)* *(Teacher and students:)* mi

Ustedes solos.
Digo /mmm/ y añado /ooo/.
¿Qué sílaba se forma? mo

Individual Practice
(Provide individual practice.)

Han hecho otro gran trabajo, ¿y saben lo que significa eso? Marcaré esta actividad en la Hoja de maestría, y pasaremos a nuestra siguiente actividad.

30 Lesson 4

Multisyllabic Words

In Multisyllabic Words, students learn to blend syllables to form a word. As you use Pepe the puppet, students listen to Pepe say the syllables in a word and then join the syllables to say the word.

Pretend to whisper a word to Pepe. Move Pepe's mouth so it seems as if he is saying each syllable: **Sa po.** *(Pause.)* **Sapo.** Ask students to listen carefully to Pepe. Pretend to whisper the word again to Pepe. **Sa po.** *(Pause.)* Say, **¿Qué palabra dijo Pepe? (What word did Pepe say?) Sapo.** Use the hand-drop cue to prompt students to respond in unison. Repeat the process with the remaining multisyllabic words.

In these auditory activities, pause and give students sufficient time to think about what they are doing in the task. Providing an instructional cue allows students to respond in unison as you monitor and observe if each student is able to hear individual phonemes that are blended to form a word or if each student is able to hear syllables within words. These are complex auditory tasks that may require scaffolding. For example, hold up a finger for each sound when building syllables. Hold up a finger for each syllable when joining syllables to form a multisyllabic word. This scaffolding technique helps students to better hear individual sounds and syllables.

Phonemic Awareness (Teacher's Editions B and C):

There are very few activities covered in Phonemic Awareness in **Teacher's Edition B** and none in **Teacher's Edition C.** The auditory activities that appear in **Teacher's Edition B** come from the Sound Discrimination category of phonemic awareness skills previously introduced in **Teacher's Edition A.** The instructional procedures are the same. Phonemic Awareness activities have evolved into Word Recognition and Spelling activities in **Teacher's Edition B.**

Activity 4

Phonological Awareness
Multisyllabic Words

(Put on Pepe the puppet.)

Pepe va a ayudarnos con esta actividad.

Pepe aún no puede hablar como nosotros. A él le gusta hablar lentamente. Necesitamos ayudarlo a decir rápidamente las palabras. Cuando Pepe hable, ustedes tienen que escuchar bien y decirme qué dijo.

Observen cómo lo hago. *(Pretend to whisper a word to Pepe. Move Pepe's mouth so it seems as if he is saying each syllable.)* *(Pepe:)* **Sa/po.** *(Pause.)*

(Teacher:) **Sapo.**

Ahora ustedes.
(Pretend to whisper a word to Pepe.)
Escuchen. *(Move Pepe's mouth so it seems as if he is saying each syllable.)*

(Pepe:) **Sa/po.** *(Pause.)*
¿Qué palabra dijo Pepe? *(Hand-drop cue.)* sapo

(Scaffold as necessary.)

Siguiente palabra.

Repeat the process with the following words: Pa/na/má, de/se/o, mos/ca, le/er, co/mer.

Individual Practice

(Provide individual practice.)

¡Buen trabajo! Terminamos esta actividad correctamente. Puedo marcar esta caja en la Hoja de maestría y podemos pasar a la siguiente actividad.

Strand Two: Letter-Sound Correspondences

SRA Intervenciones tempranas de la lectura provides daily practice in reading and writing letter-sound correspondences. Letter-sound correspondence is taught by introducing one sound at a time. No more than three letter-sound correspondences are introduced each week.

When a new letter-sound correspondence is introduced, it is taught by letter-sound only so that students don't confuse the sound with the name of the letter. In this program, the most common or frequently occurring letter-sounds are introduced first. Letters that are visually similar or that sound alike are separated by at least three other letter-sound introductions so that students can more easily distinguish them.

Accurate pronunciation of letter-sound correspondences is carefully modeled and monitored by the teacher. Continuous sounds are held or hummed two to three seconds. Stop sounds are not held; otherwise, they become distorted.

Letter-Sound Correspondences (Teacher's Edition A)

The Letter-Sound Correspondences activities in **Teacher's Edition A** come from three categories of letter-sound correspondence skills: Letter-Sound Introduction, Letter-Sound Review, and Letter-Sound Dictation. These skills are discussed more fully below in the order in which they are introduced in the intervention.

FORMATS

- Letter-Sound Introduction
  Writing the Sound
- Letter-Sound Review
- Letter-Sound Dictation

Once a letter-sound correspondence has been taught, it will be reviewed frequently. This review occurs through two formats—Letter-Sound Review and Letter-Sound Dictation. At least one of these two activities takes place in each lesson.

Tarjetas de sonidos (Sound Cards) are used to introduce letter-sound correspondences and to correct student errors in writing exercises, Letter-Sound Dictation, and Stretch and Spell.

Mm

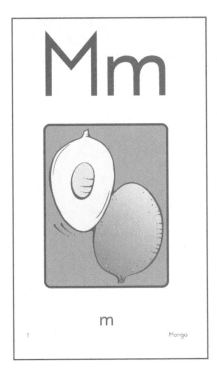

m

1   Mango

Aa

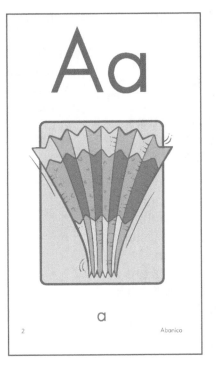

a

2   Abanico

Ll

l

4   Loro

Ch ch

ch

25   Chicharra

Tt

t

15   Tiburón

Ss

s

3   Silla

Letter-Sound Correspondences (Teacher's Edition A): Letter-Sound Introduction

Introducing Letter-Sounds

Each sound is introduced with a Sound Card that helps students associate letters with sounds. For example, the /mmm/ sound is introduced with a picture of a mango.

The first time you introduce a letter-sound correspondence, hold up the card for the letter-sound, model the sound for the letter, and ask the students to say the sound. At this time, check to make sure students are pronouncing the sounds correctly. For many of the sounds, a short poem is then read while students listen for words that have the new sound. Students then practice tracing and writing the new letter.

When a new letter-sound correspondence is introduced, it becomes part of a cumulative letter review in the next lesson. In cumulative practice, students read letter-sound correspondences they have learned in previous lessons.

ACTIVITY AT A GLANCE

- Step 1: Hold up a Sound Card and say, **El sonido de esta letra es _____ .** **(This letter's sound is_____.)** Have students say the sound first with you and then on their own. Check for mastery by giving each student a turn to read the letter-sound.

- Step 2: Read the accompanying poem, which appears both in the **Teacher's Edition** and on the back of the card, and have students listen for words that have the sound. Ask the students, **¿Cuáles palabras comienzan con el sonido _____ ?** **(What words do you hear that start with the _____ sound?)**

- Step 3: Hold up the Sound Card again, and review the sound. Point to the lowercase letter and ask, **¿Cuál es el sonido de esta letra? (What is this letter's sound?)** Then repeat with the uppercase letter.

- Step 4: Build individual mastery by having each student read the new sound.

IN THE REAL WORLD

Students enjoy listening to the short poems. Somewhere in every poem the students will be asked to repeat the sound with you. For example, **¿Qué decía Miguel cuando comía los mangos? (What did Miguel say when he ate the mangos?) /mmm/ /mmm/ /mmm/.** The students usually join in. Being playful with the students can help keep up their energy. Keep it brief, and don't let it slow the pace.

Sometimes students are not able to tell you a word from the story that begins with the target sound. Repeat the sound you want your students to listen for. Ask them to listen carefully for words that contain that sound as you reread one line from the story. Make sure you are emphasizing the sound that you want them to hear.

After introducing the letter-sound correspondence, place the Sound Card somewhere that students can see the card and where you can reference it throughout the activity.

Questions and Answers . . . .

(Review the rules quickly.)
Siéntense derechos.
Escuchen atentamente.
Contesten cuando les dé la señal.
Contesten juntos.

(Write on the marker board any letter-sounds or words students had trouble with on Assessment 2. Using the model-lead-test strategy, review the letter-sounds and words with students.)

Activity 1
Letter-Sound Introduction

Note: In this lesson, the focus is on the sound for the letter *p*, which is a stop sound. To help students read stop sounds fast, use a point-touch cue. Touch under the letter and lift your finger quickly. Then quickly touch the letter again.

*(Hold up the **Pp** Tarjeta de sonido with the capital P covered.)*

¿Cuál es el nombre de esta letra? *(Touch under p.)* p

(Provide the name of the letter to students if they don't know it.)

El sonido de esta letra es /p/. Díganlo conmigo. *(Touch under p.)*
(Teacher and students:) /p/
Otra vez. ¿Cuál es el sonido de esta letra? *(Touch under p.)* /p/

(Provide individual practice.)

La tarjeta de la *piñata* nos ayudará a recordar el sonido de la letra *p*.

Todos. ¿Cuál es el primer sonido en *piñata*? *(Touch under p.)* /p/
Cuando escribimos *piñata*, /p/ es el sonido de la primera letra. *(Point to the word piñata at the bottom of the card.)* **¡Muy bien!**

Recuerden que cada vez que aprendamos una letra, usaremos una Tarjeta de sonido para ayudarnos a recordar su sonido. Después de aprender la letra y su sonido, pondremos la Tarjeta de sonido en la pared.

Ahora voy a leer un poema. Quiero que escuchen las palabras porque algunas comienzan con el sonido /p/.

(Read the following poem.)

Pablo Pérez celebra su primer cumpleaños.
En el patio, payasos, piñatas, primos y amigos.
/p/ /p/ /p/.
Pablo le pega a la piñata,
/p/ /p/ /p/.
Todos gritan: ¡pégale! ¡pégale! ¡pégale!
Cuando le pega a la piñata el palo hace
/p/ /p/ /p/.

¿Qué sonido hace el palo cuando le pega a la piñata? *(Have students respond:)* /p/ /p/ /p/
Voy a leer el poema de nuevo. Escuchen las palabras que comienzan con el sonido /p/.

(Read the poem again, emphasizing the initial sound of words that begin with the letter p.)

¿Cuáles palabras comienzan con el sonido /p/? *(Have students respond. Possible student responses: Pablo, Pérez, primer, patio, payasos, piñatas, primos, pega, piñata, pégale, palo.)*

(Scaffold as necessary.)

*(Hold up the **Pp** Tarjeta de sonido. Uncover capital P.)*

Esta es otra forma de escribir la letra *p*. ¿Cuál es el sonido de esta letra? *(Touch under capital P.)* /p/
Esta es la *P* mayúscula. ¿Cuál es el sonido de esta letra? *(Touch under capital P.)* /p/

La *P* mayúscula se usa al principio de una oración y para escribir nombres de personas o lugares. Por ejemplo, el nombre *Pablo* empieza con *P* mayúscula.

Individual Practice
(Provide individual practice.)

Ahora vamos a poner la Tarjeta de sonido en la pared para que nos recuerde su sonido.

¡Buen trabajo encontrando las palabras que comienzan con el sonido /p/!

Han terminado esta actividad. Ahora puedo marcar la caja para esta actividad en la Hoja de maestría. Gracias por escuchar tan bien, sentarse derechos y contestar todos juntos.

Writing Letter-Sounds

After introducing a letter-sound correspondence, model writing the new letter-sound correspondence, describing each stroke as you make it. Have students trace the letter while you talk them through each pencil stroke. Students say the sound as they trace and write the sound. Saying the sound while they are writing the corresponding letter or letters is a preliminary step toward successful spelling.

Students then write the letter while saying the sound. Require students to write as neatly and as quickly as they can. Pace students in this way: **Pongan su lapiz en el punto grande. Escriban la letra _____ mientras dicen _____ . (Put your pencil on the big dot. Write the letter _____ while you say _____.)**

ACTIVITY AT A GLANCE

- Step 1: Hold up the Sound Card, and review the sound with your students.
- Step 2: Pass out pencils, and have students turn to the correct activity page. Direct students to the section on the activity sheet where they will trace and write the letter.

- Step 3: Using the marker board, model writing the new letter-sound correspondence, describing each stroke you make.
- Step 4: Students practice tracing and writing the new sound as you monitor closely for individual mastery. Students say the sound each time they trace and write the letter-sound.

IN THE REAL WORLD

If students are reluctant to say the sound while they are writing the corresponding letter-sound, this may indicate that they are not sure of the letter-sound correspondence. At first, it may help if you make the sound with them. If they write a letter without saying the sound, say, **Escríbanla mientras dicen el sonido. (Write the letter while you say the sound.)**

Monitor students closely while they are writing the letter. Stop them as soon as an error in writing begins to occur so that they don't practice an incorrect way of writing a letter. Model the letter for them again on the marker board, and then have them rewrite the letter.

Questions and Answers

Activity 2
Writing the Letter

(*Have the marker board prepared to demonstrate tracing lowercase p.*)

(*Hold up the **Pp** Tarjeta de sonido. Cover capital P.*)

¿Cuál es el nombre de esta letra? (*Touch under p.*) p
¿Cuál es el sonido de esta letra? (*Touch under p.*) /p/

Pasen a la página 17 en el *Libro de actividades A*. Vamos a aprender a escribir la letra que hace el sonido /p/. Vamos a aprender a escribir la letra *p* minúscula. Observen cómo escribo la letra *p* minúscula. (*Model, explaining each stroke you make. Use the marker board.*) **Primero pongo mi lápiz en el punto grande. Luego trazo la primera letra que hace el sonido /p/.**

(*Direct students to the first p.*)

Miren esta página del *Libro de actividades A*. Las letras en esta página están casi escritas.

Pongan su lápiz en el punto grande de la letra que hace el sonido /p/. Tracen la letra conmigo mientras dicen /p/. (*Demonstrate, and monitor.*)

Note: Walk students through strokes used to trace the letter p. Students must not be left on their own to complete a line of tracing p. Give them specific directions: **Pongan su lápiz en el punto grande. Tracen la letra mientras dicen /p/.** Continue this pattern until students have traced all the *p*'s on the first line: **Continúen hasta que hayan trazado todas las letras en el renglón.**

¡Buen trabajo trazando la letra que hace el sonido /p/!

(*Direct students to the next line.*)

En el siguiente renglón escriban la letra *p* minúscula mientras dicen el sonido /p/. (*Monitor, and correct.*)

Note: Walk students through strokes used to write the letter p. Students must not be left on their own to complete a line of writing p. Give them specific directions: **Pongan su lápiz en el punto grande. Escriban la letra mientras dicen /p/.** Continue this pattern until students have written all the *p*'s for each set of dots on the second line: **Continúen hasta que hayan escrito todas las letras en el renglón.**

(*Hold up the **Pp** Tarjeta de sonido, and uncover capital P. Have the marker board prepared to demonstrate tracing capital P. Touch under P on the card.*)

Ahora vamos a aprender a escribir la *P* mayúscula. La *p* minúscula y la *P* mayúscula tienen el mismo sonido y se escriben casi igual.

Observen cómo la escribo. (*Model, explaining each stroke you make. Use the marker board.*) **Pongo mi lápiz en el punto grande. Trazo la primera letra mayúscula que hace el sonido /p/.**

(*Direct students to the first P.*)

Miren los últimos dos renglones de esta página. Estas letras están casi escritas también.

Háganlo conmigo. Pongan su lápiz en el punto grande de la letra que hace el sonido /p/.

Tracen la letra mientras dicen el sonido /p/. (*Demonstrate, and monitor*). **Sigan trazando las letras hasta el final del renglón.**

¡Buen trabajo trazando la letra que hace el sonido /p/!

(*Direct students to the next line.*)

En el siguiente renglón escriban la letra *P* mientras dicen su sonido. Continúen hasta que hayan escrito todas las letras en el renglón.

(*Demonstrate, and monitor.*)

¡Buen trabajo escribiendo la *p* minúscula y la *P* mayúscula! Completaron esta actividad. Ahora puedo marcar la caja para esta actividad en la Hoja de maestría.

Lección 11

Pp

Actividad 2

p   p   p   p   p

p   p   p   p   p

P   P   P   P   P

P   P   P   P   P

Libro de actividades A   17

Letter Formation: Writing Letters

The main purpose of writing exercises is to reinforce the letter-to-sound correspondence. This is why students should say the sound while they write the sound. Practice writing letter-sound correspondences is foundational to the Stretch and Spell activities in the Word Recognition and Spelling Strand, where students write whole words based on the letter-sounds they have learned.

Writing exercises should not turn into handwriting lessons. It is important to keep up the pace and to encourage your students to write as accurately and quickly as they can with no erasing. Choose a writing system of your choice or specific to your school, and consistently demonstrate letter formation for students.

Letter-Sound Correspondences (Teacher's Edition A): Letter-Sound Review

After each new letter-sound correspondence is introduced, it is added to a cumulative letter-sound review. During Letter-Sound Review activities, use the point-touch cue. First, focus the students' attention on the letter by pointing to it. Then, touch under the letter to cue students to read the letter. Touch under continuous sounds for about two seconds before lifting your finger and pointing to the next letter. Tell students to hold the sound for as long as you touch under the letter-sound. For stop sounds, point-touch, and lift your finger quickly. If you do not lift quickly, students will distort the sound by adding a schwa sound; /t/ will become /tuh/.

In the first few lessons, there are directional arrows and dots underneath the letters as another visual cue for the students. The arrows and dots gradually fade. Dots reappear occasionally under a letter that is represented by a letter combination so that students will know to read the letter combination as one sound.

ACTIVITY AT A GLANCE

- Step 1: Hold up the Sound Card of the last letter-sound correspondence introduced. Review the sound for that letter with your students. **Hemos aprendido el sonido de esta letra. ¿Cuál es el sonido de esta letra? (We know this letter's sound. What is the sound of this letter?)**

- Step 2: Hold the **Teacher's Edition** at shoulder level so all students can easily see the page of letter-sounds. Tell students, **Cuando señale el punto debajo de la letra, digan su sonido y continúen diciéndolo hasta que señale el siguiente punto. (When I touch under a letter-sound, say its sound. Say its sound for as long as I touch under it.)**

- Step 3: Touch under each letter-sound. Hold your finger under continuous sounds for two to four seconds. Touch under stop sounds only briefly to emphasize that they are said quickly.

- Step 4: End with individual mastery check by having each student read three or four letter-sounds.

- Correct errors by pointing to the letter-sound that was mispronounced. Say, **El sonido de esta letra es _____ . (This letter's sound is _____ .)** Say the correct sound for students. Ask your students to repeat the sound. **¿Cuál es el sonido de esta letra? (What is this letter's sound?)** Then back up two or three letters, and begin again.

- Create a game-like quality by varying the amount of time you hold under a continuous sound during letter-sound review. This reinforces the idea that the students are supposed to hold the sound as long as you touch under it. Add a fun element by holding under the occasional continuous sound for three or four seconds, letting your eyes get big as if you know students are running out of air, and then quickly move to the next sound. Remember to always touch under a continuous sound for two or three seconds, and to always move quickly off stop sounds. Never hold a stop sound, or the sound will be distorted.

Questions and Answers

Lesson 13

(Review rules quickly.)

Siéntense derechos.
Escuchen atentamente.
Contesten cuando les dé la señal.
Contesten juntos.

Activity 1
Letter-Sound Review

Repasemos los sonidos de algunas letras.
Ustedes conocen estas letras.

(Hold up the book, and touch under the letters so all students can see them.)

Cuando señale el punto debajo de la letra, digan su sonido y continúen diciéndolo hasta que señale el siguiente punto.
Recuerden que van a decir los sonidos de las letras de la misma manera que siempre. Observen cómo lo hago. *(Touch under the first p.) /p/.*

(Touch under each letter, stopping at the dot. Vary the amount of time you touch each dot, 2–4 seconds, to create a gamelike quality. Remember to go from left to right across the page. Touch under p very quickly.)

(Use the model-lead-test strategy when a student makes a mistake.)

ERROR CORRECTION:
Mi turno. Miren y escuchen nuevamente. *(Say the sound for 2 seconds.)*
Háganlo conmigo. *(Say the sound with students.)*
Ahora, ustedes juntos. *(Students say the sound.)*
Ahora vamos a hacerlo otra vez. *(Back up 2 items and restart the activity.)*

P p. P s. A. m. L. S. a. l. P. s.

Individual Practice

(Provide individual practice with 2 letters per student.)

¡Buen trabajo diciendo los sonidos de las letras! Completaron esta actividad. Ahora puedo marcar la caja para esta actividad en la Hoja de maestría.

Arrows and Dots

In letter-sound review, students read each letter-sound as you touch under it. Initially, arrows and dots appear under the letters as an added visual cue. The arrows promote left-to-right directionality. Dots are used to differentiate sounds. The use of dots and arrows also helps students make the transition from reading individual sounds to sounding out words and reading connected text. After a few lessons, arrows and dots gradually begin to fade. Dots temporarily reappear throughout the lessons to help students remember to read certain sounds—for example, a *g* with a dot underneath. The *g* with the dot is used initially in cumulative reviews to assist students in remembering that *g* has a soft sound when followed by vowels *e* and *i*. Because Spanish sounding out is also done at the syllable level, students read words by chunking them into syllables. The syllables will appear underlined in the **Teacher's Edition:** *fru ta*. These lines will not fade. Below is a description of the progression of the curriculum from arrows and dots under letter-sounds to instances with no arrows or dots under the letter-sounds for the Letter-sound Correspondences Strand.

Visual Prompts—Fading

1. Letter-sounds first appear in the intervention with arrows and dots under each letter-sound.

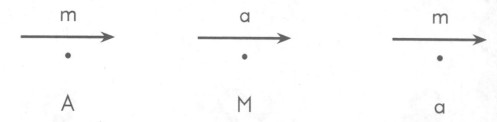

2. Starting in Lesson 11, the arrows begin to fade.

3. In Lesson 21, the dots begin to fade. Dots will reappear from time to time for letter combinations that form one letter-sound and for doubled letters as a cue to students that the letters form one sound.

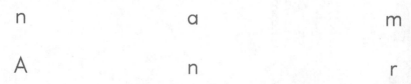

Letter-Sound Correspondences (Teacher's Edition A): Letter-Sound Dictation

Letter-Sound Dictation is a variant of cumulative letter-sound review in which students practice writing letters for sounds they have learned. Letter-Sound Dictation requires students to retrieve information, a more advanced skill than simple recognition.

ACTIVITY AT A GLANCE

- Step 1: Pass out pencils, and have students turn to the correct activity page.

- Step 2: Say to the students, **Voy a decir un sonido y ustedes van a escribir la letra que representa ese sonido. Escuchen.** *(Say the sound.)* **Pongan su lápiz en el primer espacio. Escriban la /nnn/ minúscula. Digan /nnn/ mientras escriben la letra.** (I will say a sound and you will write the letter for that sound. Put your pencil in the first space. Write the small /nnn/. Say /nnn/ while you write the letter.)

- Step 3: Dictate one sound at a time. Hold continuous sounds two seconds. Do not hold stop sounds.

- Step 4: Students say the sound as they write each letter. Check for individual mastery by monitoring students closely while they are writing the letter. If students make an error, stop them, model the letter on the board, and have students rewrite the letter correctly.

IN THE REAL WORLD

You want your students to write neatly, with no erasing, but as fast as they can.

Your students are continually reinforcing letter-sound correspondence by saying the sound each time they write the corresponding letter. Listen carefully to make sure that the sound they say matches the letter they are writing. **Has dicho /b/ pero has escrito /d/. (You said /b/, but you wrote /d/.)** Have them repeat the correct sound, and then have them write the correct letter while they say its sound.

Questions and Answers

(Review rules quickly.)

Siéntense derechos.

Escuchen atentamente.

Contesten cuando les dé la señal.

Contesten juntos.

Activity 1
Letter–Sound Dictation

Pasen a la página 23 en el *Libro de actividades A*. Miren los espacios para la actividad 1 en esta página. Ahora van a escribir algunas letras. Voy a decir un sonido y ustedes van a escribir en uno de los espacios la letra que representa ese sonido. Miren y escuchen. Mi turno. El sonido es /nnn/. ¿Cuál es la letra que hace el sonido /nnn/? *(Pause.)* **N.**

Entonces, escribo la letra *N* mayúscula. Observen cómo escribo la letra *N* mayúscula. *(Model, explaining each stroke you make. Use the marker board.)*

Ahora, háganlo conmigo. Pongan su lápiz en el primer espacio. Escriban la /nnn/ mayúscula. Digan /nnn/ mientras escriben la letra.

(Monitor, and correct.)

Pongan su lápiz en el siguiente espacio. Escriban la /nnn/ minúscula. Digan /nnn/ mientras escriben la letra.

(Monitor, and correct.)

(Use terms such as minúscula and mayúscula as appropriate.)

> Repeat the process with the following letters: **P, p, l, s, A, m.**

¡Buen trabajo escribiendo las letras! Terminamos esta actividad correctamente. Marcaré esta actividad en la Hoja de maestría.

Dejen el libro de actividades abierto porque lo usaremos más tarde.

Lección 15

Actividad 1

N   n   P   p

I   s   A   m

Actividad 2

m   n

Libro de actividades A   23

Letter-Sound Correspondences (Teacher's Edition B)

The Letter-Sound Correspondences activities presented in **Teacher's Edition B** come from the same three categories of Letter-Sound Correspondences skills previously introduced in **Teacher's Edition A:** Letter-Sound Introduction, Letter-Sound Review, and Letter-Sound Dictation. As letter-sound correspondences continue to be introduced, students practice reading letters that can be read more than one way when followed by certain vowels (e.g., the sound for *g* in the syllable *ge* as opposed to *ga*).

FORMATS

- Letter-Sound Introduction
  Writing the Sound
- Letter-Sound Review
- Letter-Sound Dictation

Letter-Sound Correspondences (Teacher's Edition B): Letter-Sound Introduction

Letters with Multiple Sounds

In the **Teacher's Edition B,** students learn how to read a letter one way and then another way. For example, the letter *g* can be read with the /j/ sound before the vowels *e* and *i*. Letter *g* has a hard sound before the vowels *a, o,* and *u.*

For example, hold up the syllable card *ge.* Touch under the letter *g* and introduce the soft *g* sound: **El sonido de esta letra aquí es /j/. Cuando la letra *e* va detrás de la g, la sílaba que se forma se lee /je/. ¿Cómo se dice? /je/ (This letter's sound here is /j/. When the letter *e* goes after g, the syllable is read /je/. How do you read this syllable?)** At the end of the lesson, ask students: **¿Cómo se lee esta sílaba? (How do you read this syllable?)**

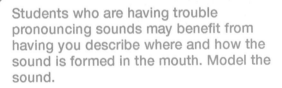

ACTIVITY AT A GLANCE

- Step 1: Hold up the syllable card.
- Step 2: Tell students the letter makes another sound. For example, students have learned the hard sound for letter the *g*. Now introduce the soft sound for *g*. Say, **Cuando la letra *e* va detrás de la g, la sílaba que se forma se lee /je/. (When the letter *e* goes after g, the syllable is read /je/.)**
- Step 3: Have students say the sound first with you and then by themselves.
- Step 4: Have students read the syllable with the soft *g* sound. **¿Cómo se lee esta sílaba? (How do we read this syllable?)**
- Step 5: Review the sound for *g* when followed by e or *i* with students.

IN THE REAL WORLD

Students who are having trouble pronouncing sounds may benefit from having you describe where and how the sound is formed in the mouth. Model the sound.

Questions and Answers

When contrasting sounds (for example, hard and soft sounds for *g*), scaffold by reviewing the sound as it was initially taught by using the sound card and reviewing the poem that was used to introduce the letter-sound.

Lesson 44

Activity 5

Letter-Sound Introduction

Part A: Letter-Sound Introduction

Vamos a aprender un sonido nuevo. Presten mucha atención.

(Hold up the Tarjeta de sílaba ge. Touch under g.)

El sonido de esta letra aquí es /j/.
¿Cuál es el sonido de esta letra? /j/
Cuando la letra e va detrás de la g, la sílaba que se forma se lee /je/.
¿Cómo se dice? /je/
Juntos. (Slide your finger under ge.)
¿Cómo se lee esta sílaba? (Teacher and students:) /je/

(Slide your finger under ge.)

Ustedes solos. ¿Cómo se lee esta sílaba? /je/

(Scaffold as necessary.)

Individual Practice

(Provide individual practice.)

Part B: Thumbs Up—Thumbs Down Game

(Hold up the Tarjeta de sílaba ge.)

Van a prestar atención a la sílaba /je/ al principio de la palabra. ¿A cuál sílaba tienen que prestar atención? /je/
¿Qué van a hacer si oyen el sonido /je/ al principio de la palabra? (Students should put their thumbs up.)

Correcto. Después que diga la palabra, apunten su pulgar hacia arriba si la palabra comienza con el sonido /je/.
Si no escuchan el sonido /je/ al principio de la palabra, entonces apunten su pulgar hacia abajo.

Listos. La primera palabra es gente.
¿Escuchan /je/ al principio de gente?
(Students should put their thumbs up.)

(Scaffold as necessary.)

¡Muy bien! Gente comienza con el sonido /je/. Bajen sus manos.

> Repeat the process with the following words: **gato, gemelas, general, llama, gallina, gema, gusta, culpa, generoso.**

Individual Practice

(Provide individual practice.)

¡Buen trabajo identificando las palabras que comienzan con el sonido /je/! Puedo marcar esta actividad en la Hoja de maestría, y podemos pasar a la siguiente actividad.

Letter-Sound Correspondence (Teacher's Edition B): Letter-Sound Review

Cumulative Practice: Multiple Spellings of the Same Sound

In Spanish, there are very few sounds that can be spelled in multiple ways. As students progress through the program, cumulative letter-sound review will include these sounds that are spelled more than one way, such as /y/, represented by *ll* or *y*. During cumulative letter review, students will practice lists that have one sound represented several ways. These items are treated like all other items using the point-touch cue.

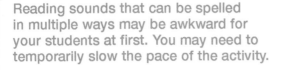

ACTIVITY AT A GLANCE

- Step 1: Begin the activity as you have in **Teacher's Edition A: Cuando señale debajo del punto de una letra, digan su sonido y continúen diciéndolo hasta que señale el siguiente punto. (When I touch under the dot, say the letter's sound and continue saying it until I touch the next dot.)**

- Step 2: End with an individual mastery check by having each student read three or four sounds.

IN THE REAL WORLD

Reading sounds that can be spelled in multiple ways may be awkward for your students at first. You may need to temporarily slow the pace of the activity.

If students are not able to remember that several letters can represent the same sound, treat it as an error. Tell the students the sound, then back up two or more letters, and begin again.

Questions and Answers

Lesson 56

(Write on the marker board any letter-sounds or words students had trouble with on Assessment 11. Using the model-lead-test strategy, review the letter-sounds and words with students.)

Activity 1
Letter-Sound Review

Van a repasar los sonidos de algunas de las letras que hemos aprendido hasta ahora.

(Hold up the book so all students can see the letters.)

Ustedes conocen estas letras.
Cuando señale una letra, digan su sonido.

(Touch under the first y.)
¿Cuál es el sonido? /yyy/
¿Cuál es la letra? y

¡Muy bien!

(Scaffold as necessary.)

(Touch under each letter. Vary the amount of time you touch under each letter to create a gamelike quality. Remember to go from left to right across the page.)

Repeat the process with the remaining letter-sounds.

Individual Practice

(Provide individual practice with 4 or 5 sounds per student.)

¡Muy buen trabajo diciendo los sonidos y las letras! Ahora puedo marcar esta actividad en la Hoja de maestría, y podemos pasar a la siguiente actividad.

Letter-Sound Correspondences (Teacher's Edition B): Letter-Sound Dictation

Sounds with Multiple Spellings

Once students learn sounds that can be written in more than one way, they will be expected during Letter-Sound Dictation activities to write all the alternate ways they have learned. When dictating a sound that can be written more than one way, say, **Escriban la(s) letra(s) que corresponde(n) al sonido _____ . Ahora, escriban otra(s) letra(s) que corresponde(n) al sonido _____ . (Write the letter(s) that correspond(s) to the sound _____ . Now write the other letter(s) that correspond(s) to the sound _____ .)**

ACTIVITY AT A GLANCE

- Step 1: Begin letter-sound dictation as usual. **Van a escribir las letras de los sonidos que les voy a dictar. (You are going to write the letters for the sounds that I will dictate.)**

- Step 2: When you say a sound that can be written more than one way, remind your students to write the sound in another way.

- Step 3: Correct all errors as they occur, checking for individual mastery.

IN THE REAL WORLD

Use the Sound Cards to remind students how a sound is written or of alternate spellings they may have forgotten to write.

Questions and Answers

Lesson 75

Activity 2
Letter-Sound Dictation

Pasen a la página 71 en el *Libro de actividades B*.

Van a escribir las letras de los sonidos que les voy a dictar. Listos. El primer sonido es /ch/.

Escriban las letras que corresponden al sonido /ch/. Digan /ch/ mientras escriben las letras.

(Monitor, and correct.)

¿Qué letras escribieron? ch

Pongan su lápiz en el siguiente espacio. Escriban las letras que corresponden al sonido /rr/. Digan /rr/ mientras escriben la letra.

¿Qué letras escribieron? rr

(Monitor, and correct.)

Repeat the process with the following sounds: /b/, /ñi/, */j/ (ji, ge, gi), /v/, */y/ (y, ll), */k/ (k, q).

(Monitor, correct, and scaffold as necessary.)

Note: With these sounds, tell the students to write it one way and then to write it all other ways they know.

¡Muy buen trabajo escribiendo los sonidos! Ahora puedo marcar la caja para esta actividad en la Hoja de maestría.

Dejen el libro de actividades abierto porque lo usaremos más tarde.

Nombre_____

Lección 75

Actividad 2

ch	rr
b	ñ
j	ge
gi	v
y	ll
k	qu

Copyright © The McGraw-Hill Companies, Inc.

Letter-Sound Correspondence (Teacher's Edition C)

Letter-Sound Correspondences activities that continue in **Teacher's Edition C** continue as introduced and practiced in **Teacher's Editions A** and **B,** with Letter-Sound Introduction, Letter-Sound Review, and Letter-Sound Dictation activities.

Strand Three: Word Recognition and Spelling

In Word Recognition and Spelling activities, students begin looking at whole words and applying the skills they have learned in the Phonemic Awareness and Letter-Sound Correspondences strands to read and spell these words.

As students progress across lessons, words they read become increasingly complex. In the beginning, students are asked to read only two- and three-phoneme words consisting of closed syllable, VCV (vowel-consonant-vowel) and CVC (consonant-vowel-consonant) patterns. To facilitate students' ability to sound out and easily read these initial words, the first letter in each word represents a continuous sound. From this initial stage, words gradually increase in complexity until students are easily reading multisyllabic words.

Sounding out words may be difficult for students in the beginning. To facilitate the process, the words for Sounding Out activities will consist only of letter-sounds that have been previously taught. The skill is practiced with a few words each day.

In Spanish, because of the syllabic nature of the language, considerable attention is given to sounding out and reading syllables. This occurs in **Teacher's Editions A** and **B.** Students also sound out words sound by sound. Students then move to reading syllables quickly and then reading words by syllables. For example, students are told to think about the sounds in the syllable before reading it quickly. Similarly, students are told to think about the sounds in a word before reading it quickly. When students read the syllable or a word quickly, this is explained as "reading fast first" (for example, Lesson 18, Activity 2 and Lesson 27, Activity 6). Students rapidly move into decoding words syllable by syllable.

The Sounding Out format changes quickly. First, students only sound out the word. Next, they sound out the word, and then read it. Lessons quickly progress from having students read a list of words by Sounding Out and Reading Fast to reading the words in the list a second time fast first, without sounding out the word aloud. By the end of **Teacher's Edition C,** students are required to Read Fast First, without sounding out words.

SOUNDING OUT AT A GLANCE

Sounding Out

a m a

• • •

- Very difficult in the beginning
- Words to sound out contain only mastered sounds
- Practiced a little every day
- Moves quickly to chunking and then to Reading Fast First

Sound It Out

Changes quickly

1. Sounding out syllables and words by phonemes.
2. Sounding out the word by syllables and then reading the word.
3. Sounding out the word, and then reading the word again fast
4. Reading the word fast first

Sound Out in the Beginning

Format:

1. Hold up the **Teacher's Edition** so students can see the list.
2. Tell students to sound out the first word.
3. Touch under each sound while students say each sound in the word.
4. Touch under continuous sounds for two seconds, but move quickly off stop sounds.
5. When sounding out by syllables, touch under each underlined syllable and then read the word.

Sounding-Out Format

1. Sound by Sound

   "Cuando señale debajo del punto de la letra, digan su sonido y continúen diciéndolo hasta que señale la siguiente letra. No se detengan entre los sonidos, Díganlos de corrido."

   m a s a
   • • • •

2. Syllable by Syllable

   Lean la sílaba. *(Slide your finger under the syllable.)* **ma**

   Lean la sílaba. *(Slide your finger under the syllable.)* **pa**

   Lean la palabra. *(Slide your finger under the word.)* **mapa**

   ma pa

Word Recognition and Spelling (Teacher's Edition A)

The Word Recognition and Spelling activities presented in **Teacher's Edition A** come from three categories of word recognition and spelling skills: Sounding Out, High-Frequency Words, and Stretch and Spell, which are discussed more fully below in the order in which they are introduced in the program.

FORMATS

- Sounding Out

  Sounding Out in the Beginning Lessons
  Sounding Out and Reading Fast
  What Syllable Now?
  Forming Plurals
  Reading Fast First
  Multisyllabic Chunking

- High-Frequency Words, New and Review
- Stretch and Spell
- Sentence Writing

Word Recognition and Spelling (Teacher's Edition A): Sounding Out

Sounding Out in the Beginning

All Sounding Out activities are presented initially using the **Teacher's Edition.** Initially, students sound out words and syllables sound by sound. To present these activities, hold the **Teacher's Edition** at shoulder level so all students can see the word list. Tell students to sound out the first word. Guide students by touching under each letter-sound while they say each sound in the word.

When students are sounding out words or syllables sound by sound, touch under continuous sounds for two or three seconds, but move off stop sounds quickly. A word or syllable being sounded out should sound like a word or syllable being stretched. There should be no pauses between sounds. In the early lessons, directional arrows and dots appear underneath the words as visual cues.

These arrows and dots fade quickly. Dots reappear occasionally under a new letter-sound correspondence that is represented by a letter combination or when letters are doubled so that students know to read the letter combination as one sound.

Initially, Sounding Out activities are led by the teacher. However, eventually they are student led. In student-led activities, students are taught to touch under each sound in the word as they sound it out. After sounding the word out, students read the word. These tasks are important because they teach students to eventually sound out words independently.

ACTIVITY AT A GLANCE

- Step 1: Hold up the **Teacher's Edition** with the word list.
- Step 2: Tell students to sound out the first word.
- Step 3: Touch under each letter-sound while the students say the sounds in the word.
- Step 4: Touch under continuous sounds for two seconds, but move quickly off stop sounds.
- Step 5: Repeat the procedure with the remaining words.
- Step 6: End with individual mastery check by having students sound out one or two words each.

IN THE REAL WORLD

Students tend to rush their sounds when they first learn to sound out words. It is very important for you to model holding continuous sounds for two to three seconds. It is equally important to make sure that your students are holding the sound for as long as you touch under the letter-sound. You may need to stop students and remind them that they need to stay together and that they need to say the sound as long as you touch under the letter-sound. Then start them again. Holding continuous sounds makes sounding out easier for students. If you teach students to do this correctly in the beginning, they will be better able to handle reading word lists and connected text later in the intervention. Move off stop sounds quickly.

Questions and Answers

Activity 6
Sounding Out
Syllables

Note: Follow this format:
1. Move your finger under first letter: **/mmm/**.
2. Touch under the letter for 1.5 seconds and say the sound.
3. Move to the next letter: **/aaa/**. Hold for 1.5 seconds. Remember to slide from one letter to the next.
4. Say the syllable slowly.

En esta actividad vamos a aprender cómo decir sílabas sonido por sonido. Voy a leer una sílaba sonido por sonido siguiendo de izquierda a derecha. Miren y escuchen. (Demonstrate.) **La sílaba es ma. Digo los sonidos /mmm/aaa/. Leo la sílaba. Ma.**

(Hold up the book so all students can see ma. Slowly slide your finger under the syllable, moving from dot to dot.)

Ahora, háganlo conmigo. Cuando señale debajo de la letra, digan su sonido y sigan diciéndolo hasta que señale la siguiente letra. No se detengan entre los sonidos. Díganlos de corrido. Listos. Digamos los sonidos. (Slide your finger under each letter of ma.)
(Teacher and students:) **/mmm/aaa/**

Ahora, ustedes solos. Digan lentamente los sonidos sin detenerse. Después, lean la sílaba. Luego, léanla rápidamente. Listos.
(Touch under the first letter of ma, /mmm/, for 1.5 seconds.)

Digan el sonido. /mmm/
(Touch under the second letter, /aaa/, for 1.5 seconds.)

Digan el sonido. /aaa/
Lean la sílaba. (Slide your finger under the syllable.) ma
Otra vez. Léanla. (Quickly slide your finger under the syllable.) ma

(Scaffold as necessary.)

Siguiente.

| Repeat the process with sa. |

Individual Practice
(Provide individual practice.)

¡Buen trabajo diciendo las sílabas sonido por sonido! Terminamos otra actividad. Ahora puedo marcar la caja para esta actividad en la Hoja de maestría.

Activity 7
Sounding Out
Student Led

Miren la página 22 en el *Libro de actividades A.*

En esta actividad van a leer las palabras sonido por sonido como les voy a indicar. Levanto el dedo índice y lo pongo debajo del primer punto de la palabra. *(Demonstrate.)*

Luego muevo el dedo de punto a punto, diciendo los sonidos. *(Demonstrate as you do the process.)*

Mi turno. /Mmm/aaa/lll/.

Note: Remember to slide your finger from one dot to the next.

Muevo rápidamente el dedo por los puntos mientras leo la palabra. *(Slide your finger under the word as fast as you say it.)* **Mal.**

Háganlo conmigo.

Miren las palabras para la actividad 7 en el *Libro de actividades A.*

Levanten el dedo índice y pónganlo debajo del primer punto de la palabra. *(Monitor.)*

Muevan el dedo de punto a punto diciendo el sonido cuando escuchen el golpecito. Listos. *(Tap for each letter. Students should slowly slide their finger under the word, moving from dot to dot as they sound out the word.)*

(Teacher and students:) **/mmm/aaa/lll/**

Muevan rápidamente el dedo por los puntos mientras leen. Leamos la palabra rápidamente cuando oigamos un golpecito. Ahora leamos la palabra. *(Tap once for the whole word. Students should slide their finger under the word as fast as they say it.)* *(Teacher and students:)* **mal**

(Scaffold as necessary.)

Ahora, ustedes solos. *(Pause.)* **Pongan el índice en el primer punto de la palabra.** *(Monitor.)* **Digan cada sonido.** *(Tap for each letter. Students should slide their finger under the word, moving from dot to dot as they sound out the word.)* **/mmm/aaa/lll/**

Lean la palabra. *(Tap once for the whole word. Students should slide their finger under the word as fast as they say it.)* **mal**

(Scaffold as necessary.)

Note: Write the words *mal, mala, sal, sala, la sala,* and *papá* on the marker board. If students cannot move their finger as they sound out the words, demonstrate how to do it. If they still can't do it, then prompt students by gently guiding their hands, helping them move a finger from dot to dot as they sound out the word. Before touching students, explain that you are going to guide their hands and physically help: **Yo los voy a ayudar físicamente guiándoles las manos.**

Siguiente palabra.
Pongan su dedo en el primer punto debajo de la palabra. Listos. *(Tap for each letter. Students should slide their finger under the word, moving from dot to dot as they sound out the word.)* **/mmm/aaa/lll/aaa/**

(Scaffold as necessary.)

Lean la palabra. *(Tap once for the whole word. Students should slide their finger under the word as fast as they say it.)* **mala**

(Scaffold as necessary.)

> **Repeat the process with the following words: sal, sala, la sala, papá.**

Individual Practice
(Provide individual practice.)

¡Buen trabajo leyendo las palabras sonido por sonido! Han hecho otra parte de la lección perfectamente. Marcaré esta actividad en la Hoja de maestría.

Sounding Out and Reading Fast

Sounding Out and Reading Fast is an activity that begins early in **Teacher's Edition A.** Students sound out Spanish words sound by sound before reading the word. To teach this format, hold the **Teacher's Edition** at shoulder level, and tell students to sound out the word. Students say each sound as you touch under the letter or letter combination. As always, you touch under continuous sounds for approximately two seconds but move off stop sounds quickly. Students then read the word. Repeat this procedure with the remaining words. End with individual practice of one to two words per student to assess for individual mastery.

ACTIVITY AT A GLANCE

- Step 1: Hold up the **Teacher's Edition** with the word list.
- Step 2: Tell students to sound out the word.
- Step 3: Touch under each sound while the students say each sound in the word.
- Step 4: Touch under continuous sounds for two seconds but move quickly off stop sounds.
- Step 5: Ask students to read the word fast.
- Step 6: Repeat the procedure with the remaining words.
- Step 7: End with individual mastery check by having students read one or two words each.

IN THE REAL WORLD

It is easier for students to blend and read the word fast if they hum the individual sounds as they sound out the word. In order to hum as they sound out, students should hold the continuous sounds. In this way, holding continuous sounds, as introduced in the Phonemic Awareness and Letter-Sound Correspondences strands, enables your students to read words.

If your students are having trouble blending the word, it may be because you are moving too quickly from sound to sound and not holding continuous sounds long enough. Slow the sounding-out pace a little to see if this makes a difference for students. Once they can sound out the word and read it fast, smoothly, and without error, pick up the pace.

Questions and Answers

Lesson 11

Activity 7
Sounding Out

Note: Follow this format:

1. Move your finger under first letter: /lll/.
2. Touch under the letter for 1.5 seconds and say the sound.
3. Move to the next letter: /aaa/. Hold for 1.5 seconds. Remember to slide from one letter to the next.
4. Say the word slowly.

Vamos a leer palabras sonido por sonido. Cuando señale debajo de la primera letra, digan su sonido y continúen diciéndolo hasta que señale la siguiente letra.

Primera palabra. *(Hold up the book so all students can see the words.)* **Mi turno. Observen cómo lo hago.** *(Touch under each letter, moving your finger along the word.)* /Lll/aaa/.

¿Qué palabra leí? *La.*

Ahora, ustedes solos. *(Touch under each letter, moving your finger along the word.)* /lll/aaa/

¿Qué palabra leyeron? la

(Scaffold as necessary.)

Siguiente palabra.

Repeat the process with the remaining words.

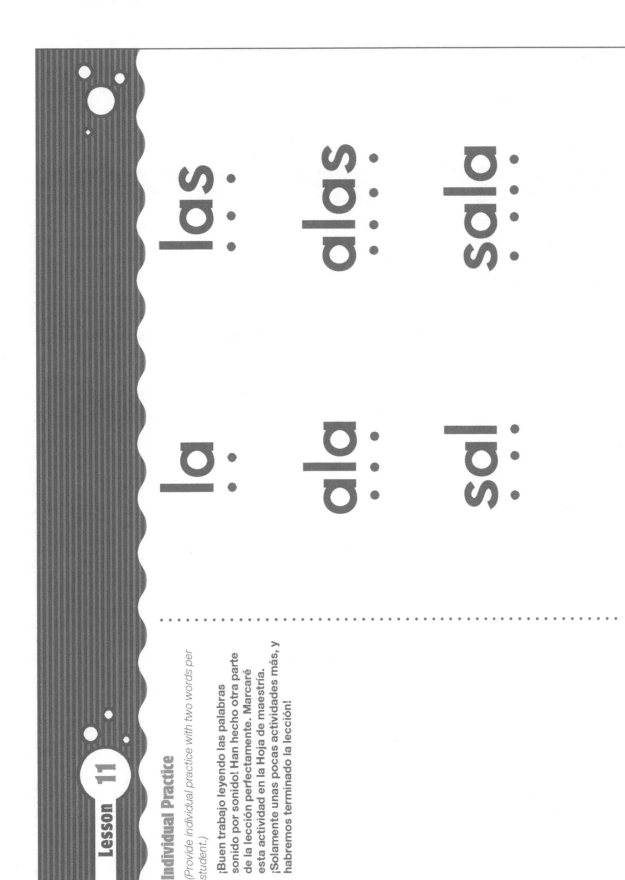

Individual Practice

(Provide individual practice with two words per student.)

¡Buen trabajo leyendo las palabras sonido por sonido! Han hecho otra parte de la lección perfectamente. Marcaré esta actividad en la Hoja de maestría. ¡Solamente unas pocas actividades más, y habremos terminado la lección!

la   las

ala   alas

sal   sala

91 Lesson 11

What Syllable Now?

The purpose of the What Syllable Now? activity is to teach students to construct and read syllables by omitting or adding a consonant or vowel to create a new syllable.

Later, in **Teacher's Edition B,** this activity is expanded to include What Word Now? In What Word Now? activities, students learn that you change a word by adding or omitting a syllable.

ACTIVITY AT A GLANCE

- Step 1: Write letters on the marker board: m_ s_ l_ p_ n_ d_
- Step 2: Add a letter in the first space.
- Step 3: Slide your finger under the syllable. Students read the syllable (for example, *ma*).

- Step 4: Repeat the procedure for the remaining syllables.
- Step 5: Provide individual practice for students to read all the syllables.

IN THE REAL WORLD

Students seldom experience difficulty with this activity. They often find it fun. This activity moves quickly and should not take up much time. Nevertheless, it is a valuable exercise. If students do experience trouble with the activity, this may indicate that they need additional practice Stretching and Blending and Sounding Out and Reading Fast.

Questions and Answers

Lesson 23

Activity 4
What Syllable Now? Game
Building Syllables

Note: Have ready the marker board with the following letters written on it:

m_ s_ l_ p_ n_ d_

Vamos a jugar a "¿Qué sílaba es ahora?".
Observen lo que está escrito en el pizarrón. Ustedes conocen los sonidos de estas letras.
Voy a añadir una letra en el espacio y ustedes van a leer la sílaba que se forma.
Añadiré /aaa/ en el espacio. *(Write a after m.)*
Lean la sílaba. *(Slide your finger under ma.)* ma

(Scaffold as necessary.)

Repeat the process with the following syllables: sa, la, pa, na, da.

Individual Practice

(Provide individual practice with all the syllables.)

Si quito /aaa/ y añado /eee/, ¿qué sílaba se forma? *(Erase a and write e after m.)*
Lean la sílaba. *(Slide your finger under me,)* me

(Scaffold as necessary.)

Repeat the process with the following syllables: se, le, pe, ne, de.

Individual Practice

(Provide individual practice with all the syllables.)

Si quito /eee/ y añado /ooo/, ¿qué sílaba se forma? *(Erase e and write o after m.)*
Lean la sílaba. *(Slide your finger under mo.)* mo

Repeat the process with the following syllables: so, lo, po, no, do.

Individual Practice

(Provide individual practice with all the syllables.)

¡Buen trabajo! Marcaré la caja para esta actividad en la Hoja de maestría.

189 **Lesson 23**

Forming Plurals

This skill is taught within the Chunking format. Students chunk words into syllables and then read the word fast. The plural ending, -s, is added to the end of the word. Students then chunk the word again and read the new word.

ACTIVITY AT A GLANCE

- Step 1: Have the marker board ready with words from the lesson written on it: *mesa, amigo, amiga, mercado, pescado.*
- Step 2: Students touch under and read each syllable.
- Step 3: Students read the word fast.
- Step 4: Add -s to the base word to form the plural, as in the word *mesas.*
- Step 5: Students touch under and read each syllable again.
- Step 6: Students read the new word.
- Step 7: Repeat the reading routine as described above with the remaining words.
- Step 8: End with individual mastery check by having students read both the singular and the plural form of a word.

IN THE REAL WORLD

If students have trouble pronouncing the plural, ask for the answer in sentence form. For example, **Yo tengo una mesa. Yo tengo dos mesas. (I have one table. I have two tables.)** Then repeat the exercise until they can read the words in isolation.

Questions and Answers

Lesson 36

Activity 6
Plural Words

(Write mesa, amigo, amiga, mercado, and pescado on the marker board.)

Hoy vamos a leer unas palabras en plural. La mayoría de las palabras en plural tienen la letra s al final. Veamos las siguientes palabras en el pizarrón.
Mi turno. *Me (pause)* **sa.**
Leo rápidamente. *Mesa.*
(Hold one finger in the air to indicate only one.)

Si añado una s al final de la palabra, entonces estoy indicando que hay más de una mesa.
Observen cómo lo hago. *(Add an s to the end of mesa.)* **Añado la s al final de *mesa.***
Mi turno. *Me* (pause) **sas.**
Leo rápidamente. *Mesas.*
Háganlo conmigo. *(Erase the s at the end of mesas.)*
Leamos. *(Slide your finger under me.) (Teacher and students:)* me
Leamos. *(Slide your finger under sa.) (Teacher and students:)* sa
Leamos la palabra. *(Slide your finger under the entire word. Teacher and students:)* mesa
(Scaffold as necessary.)

Ahora añado una s al final de la palabra *mesa.*
Leamos la palabra. *(Teacher and students:)* mesas
(Scaffold as necessary.)
Siguiente palabra.

> **Repeat the process with the following words: amigo, amiga, mercado, pescado.**

Individual Practice
(Provide individual practice.)

¡Buen trabajo leyendo las palabras! Marcaré esta actividad en la Hoja de maestría.

282 Lesson 36

Word Recognition and Spelling (Teacher's Edition A): Reading Fast First

Once students have demonstrated competence in sounding out syllables and words and reading them fast, they learn that they don't have to sound out everything.

As a first step toward reading words automatically, without sounding out, students learn to read syllables fast using **Tarjetas de sílabas** (Syllable Cards). Students look at a syllable card and think about the sounds before reading the syllable fast. This process is then used for reading words fast. Teach students to sound out words in their heads before reading the word aloud. In these activities, control how much time students are allowed to sound out in their heads by using an auditory cue. Over time, allow less and less think time until students are reading syllables or words automatically. Eventually, Reading Fast First will require students to read syllables that are presented in the **Teacher's Edition.**

ACTIVITY AT A GLANCE

- Step 1: Students sound out a syllable or word in their heads as you touch under each letter.
- Step 2: Give students one or two seconds of think time, and then cue them to read the word.
- Step 3: Repeat the procedure with the remaining syllables or words.

- Step 4: End with individual mastery check by having students read two or three words syllables or each. When presenting syllables in the **Teacher's Edition,** allow each student to read one or two rows of syllables.

IN THE REAL WORLD

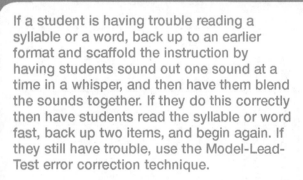

If a student is having trouble reading a syllable or a word, back up to an earlier format and scaffold the instruction by having students sound out one sound at a time in a whisper, and then have them blend the sounds together. If they do this correctly then have students read the syllable or word fast, back up two items, and begin again. If they still have trouble, use the Model-Lead-Test error correction technique.

Once enough syllables have been introduced, "El juego de las tarjetas" ("The Card Game") is introduced to increase motivation for students during syllable review. In this game the students score a point for every syllable they read correctly, and you score a point for every word read incorrectly. The students take great pleasure in trying to beat the teacher. At the same time, students are developing automatic recognition of syllables.

Questions and Answers

Activity 4
Reading Fast First
Syllables

(Have ready Tarjetas de sílabas 1–12.)

Pasamos a otra actividad. Vamos a leer sílabas. Les daré tiempo para pensar en los sonidos de la sílaba y luego la leerán rápidamente.

Mi turno. *(Hold up ma.)* **Pienso.** *(Move your lips as if you are saying ma while sliding your finger under the syllable, but make no sound.)* *(Pause 1.5 seconds.)*
Leo rápidamente. *(Quickly slide your finger under the syllable.)* **ma**

Ustedes solos. Piensen en los sonidos.
Lean la sílaba rápidamente. *(Quickly slide your finger under the syllable.)* **ma**

(Scaffold as necessary.)

Siguiente. *(Hold up me.)* **Piensen en los sonidos.**
Lean la sílaba rápidamente. *(Quickly slide your finger under the syllable.)* **me**

(Scaffold as necessary.)

Repeat the process with all syllables.

Individual Practice

(Provide individual practice.)

¡Buen trabajo leyendo sílabas! Terminamos esta actividad. Marcaré la Hoja de maestría, y podemos pasar a la siguiente parte de nuestra lección.

157 Lesson 19

ma

1

me

6

Lesson 33

cle   cli   clo

cra   cre   cro

dra   dre   dri

el   al   es   un

....

Activity 2
Reading Fast First
Syllables

(Hold up the book so all students can see the letters.)

Van a leer sílabas. Primero piensen en los sonidos y luego lean la sílaba.
(Touch under the first syllable, cle. Allow 2 seconds of think time.)

¿Cuál es la sílaba? Piensen. *(Pause.)*
Lean la sílaba. *(Slide your finger under cle.)* cle
(Scaffold as necessary.)

Siguiente sílaba.

Repeat the process with the remaining syllables: **cli, clo, cra, cre, cro, dra, dre, dri, el, al, es, un.**

Individual Practice

(Provide individual practice, having each student read one row of syllables.)

260 Lesson 33

Staff Development Guide, Spanish

87

fi   fa   fo

fe

is   in   ir

ra   an   al

ri   re   ro

ar   er

(Hold up the book, and touch under the syllable fi.)

Van a leer más sílabas. Piensen. *(Pause.)*
Lean la sílaba. (Slide your finger under fi.) fi
(Scaffold as necessary.)
Siguiente sílaba.

Repeat the process with the remaining syllables: fa, fo, fe, in, ir, is, an, al, ra, re, ro, ri, ar, er.

Individual Practice

(Provide individual practice, having each student read 2 rows of syllables.)

Ahora van a leer juntos todas las sílabas de arriba abajo. Tocaré cada sílaba y ustedes van a leerla.

Individual Practice

(Provide individual practice, having each student read one column of syllables.)

¡Excelente! Ahora puedo marcar esta actividad en la Hoja de maestría, y podemos pasar a la siguiente actividad.

261 Lesson 33

Reading Fast First—Reduced Think Time

Think time provides the time necessary for students to sound out a word in their heads before they read the word. The amount of think time specified within the lesson is the maximum amount of time allowed between words. If students can sound out words in their heads and read the words faster than the specified think time, you can move the students faster. Pace students as fast as they can read. However, if many errors start to occur, allow more think time. The lowest-performing student determines the pace.

Mastery occurs if students can meet at least the specified maximum think time. The specified criterion must be met by the group.

Moving from Teacher-Led to Student-Led

Word Recognition and Spelling activities are first presented as teacher-led activities. After students have gained proficiency in reading words with the teacher leading the activity, students begin to read words more independently. Student-led word recognition activities appear as word lists in the **Activity Books.**

In student-led activities the students themselves touch under each letter as they sound out the words while you control the pace by softly tapping on the table. The goal for all activities is for the students to read words as accurately and as independently as possible.

Lesson 13

Activity 4
Sounding Out
Chunking—Teacher Led

Note: In this activity, the object is for students to read words by chunking them into syllables, and then reading the words fast. Stretching the sounds will be used to help scaffold.

**Ahora vamos a formar palabras con las sílabas. Las palabras se forman de una o más sílabas.
Mi turno.**

Leo la palabra sílaba por sílaba. Escuchen. Leo la sílaba. (Hold up the book so all students can see the words. Slide your finger under ma.) **Ma.**
Leo la sílaba. (Slide your finger under pa.) **Pa.**
La leo rápidamente. (Quickly slide your finger under the entire word.) **Mapa.**

Háganlo conmigo. Leamos la sílaba. (Slide your finger under ma.)
(Teacher and students:) ma
Leamos la sílaba. (Slide your finger under pa.)
(Teacher and students:) pa

Leámosla rápidamente. (Quickly slide your finger under the entire word.) mapa
(Teacher and students:) mapa

(Scaffold as necessary.)

Ustedes solos. Lean la sílaba. (Slide your finger under ma.) ma
Lean la sílaba. (Slide your finger under pa.) pa
Léanla rápidamente. (Quickly slide your finger under the entire word.) mapa

¡Muy bien!
Siguiente palabra.

> **Repeat the process for the words: mala, masa, sala, Lala.**

(Scaffold as necessary.)

Individual Practice

(Provide individual practice with 1 word per student.)

¡Buen trabajo! Completaron esta actividad correctamente. Marcaré la Hoja de maestría, y podemos pasar a la siguiente parte de nuestra lección.

mapa

mala

masa

sala

Lala

Word Recognition and Spelling (Teacher's Edition A): High-Frequency Words

High-Frequency Words

High-frequency words are words that are introduced because students have not yet learned all the letter-sounds within the word. These words are introduced early because students need to know the word for a story they will be reading. Later, the unfamiliar letters and sounds are taught in a future lesson.

High-frequency words are provided for you. Each card has a number on the front to help you organize. After each **Tarjeta de palabras de uso frecuente** (High-Frequency Word Card) is introduced, students practice tracing, copying, and reading the word. Then each word is added to the deck of cards for review. High-frequency words are reviewed in nearly every lesson. Automatic recognition of these words is necessary to promote fluent reading.

ACTIVITY AT A GLANCE

- Step 1: Review high-frequency words by holding them up one at a time and saying, **¿Cuál es esta palabra? (What is this word?)**
- Step 2: Introduce the new word by holding up the card and saying, **Esta palabra es _____ . (This word is _____ .)**
- Step 3: Point to the new word, and ask your students, **¿Cuál es esta palabra? (What is this word?)**
- Step 4: Model writing the new word. Say the word as you write the word.
- Step 5: Direct students to their activity sheets, and cue students to trace the word as they say the word.
- Step 6: After they have traced the word, cue students to copy the word as they say the word.
- Step 7: End with individual mastery check by letting each student read two or three words.

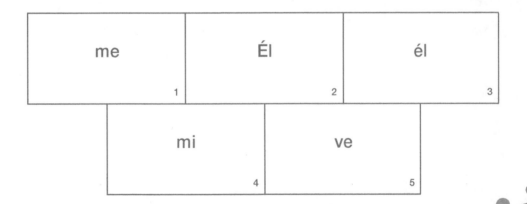

IN THE REAL WORLD

Having students say the word while they trace and copy the word further develops automatic word recognition of the new word.

If a high-frequency word is read incorrectly during review, tell students the word, have

them read it together, put the card back in the deck, and give students another chance to read the word. Try to include any missed words in the individual mastery check.

Questions and Answers

Activity 4
High-Frequency Words

(Have ready Tarjeta de palabras de uso frecuente—me.)

En esta actividad aprenderemos a leer una palabra frecuente. Las llamamos palabras frecuentes porque las verán a menudo en lo que leen. Deben poder leer las palabras frecuentes rápidamente sin decirlas sonido por sonido. Hoy aprenderán una palabra frecuente.

(Hold up Tarjeta de palabras de uso frecuente—me.)

Esta palabra es me. Digan la palabra conmigo. *(Slide your finger under me.) (Teacher and students:)* **me**

Otra vez. ¿Cuál es esta palabra? me
Lean la palabra conmigo. *(Slide your finger under me.) (Teacher and students:)* me

¿Qué dirán cada vez que vean esta palabra en una lectura? me

¡Muy bien!

(Scaffold as necessary.)

Individual Practice

(Provide individual practice.)

(Have the marker board prepared to demonstrate tracing the word me.)

Miren los espacios para la actividad 4 en la página 3 en el *Libro de actividades A*. Ahora vamos a escribir me.

Observen cómo escribo me. *(Model, explaining each stroke you make. Use the marker board.)*

Primero pongo mi lápiz en el punto grande. Luego trazo la letra m. Luego pongo mi lápiz en el siguiente punto grande y trazo la letra e.

(Demonstrate.)

Háganlo conmigo. Pongan su lápiz en el punto grande. Tracen y digan me mientras escriben. En el siguiente espacio tracen la palabra me.

(Demonstrate, and monitor.)

Note: Monitor and scaffold as necessary. Students must not be left on their own to complete a line of tracing me. Direct them to the next me to trace and give them specific directions: **Pongan su lápiz en el punto grande. Tracen me mientras dicen me.** Continue this pattern until students have traced the word me for each space on this line: **Continúen hasta que hayan trazado me en todos los espacios de este renglón.**

Ahora juntos. Siguiente renglón. Escriban la palabra me otra vez.

Pongan su lápiz en el punto grande en el primer espacio del siguiente renglón. Digan me mientras escriben.

Note: Scaffold as necessary. Students must not be left on their own to complete a line of writing me. Give them specific directions: **Pongan su lápiz en el punto grande. Escriban me mientras dicen me.** Continue this pattern until students have written the word me for each space of this line: **Continúen hasta que hayan escrito me en todos los espacios del siguiente renglón.**

¡Buen trabajo!
Han hecho otra parte de la lección perfectamente. Marcaré esta actividad en la Hoja de maestría. ¡Solamente unas pocas actividades más y habremos terminado con toda la lección!

Nombre

Lección 2

Actividad 3

m

M

m
m
m

me me me me

me me me me

Actividad 4

Libro de actividades A

3

Word Recognition and Spelling (Teacher's Edition A): Stretch and Spell

The Stretch and Blend and Letter-Sound Dictation activities students have been practicing are preparing them for spelling words. As noted with Letter-Sound Dictation, it is easier for students to look at a letter and say the sound it represents than it is for them to hear a sound and then write the letter that represents that sound.

In Stretch and Spell activities, students spell words by stretching the word and listening for each individual sound they hear in the word. As the students listen for the individual sounds, they write each sound in the order that they hear it.

The progression of Stretch and Spell mirrors the progression of Sounding Out. At first the students are stretching the words aloud while they write them. Eventually students stretch a spelling word in their heads before they spell it.

Stretch and Spell

In this format students stretch words and then spell them. Say a word, and have students stretch the word. Then have students write each sound in the correct order. On your cue, students read the word aloud.

If a student misspells a word, ask the student to stretch the word as he or she looks at what they have written. If the student has trouble stretching a word, you may need to model stretching the word.

ACTIVITY AT A GLANCE

- Step 1: Say the word.
- Step 2: Students stretch the word.
- Step 3: Students write each sound in the correct order.

- Step 4: Students read the word they spelled.
- Step 5: Repeat the procedure with the remaining words.

IN THE REAL WORLD

Use **Tarjetas de sonidos** to prompt students when necessary.

Questions and Answers

Lesson 20

Activity 2
Stretch and Spell

(Have the marker board ready to demonstrate writing words.)

Preparémonos para escribir.
Voy a decir una palabra y ustedes van a estirarla y escribirla.

Escuchen. *Es.* *(Pause.)*
Estiremos es. *(Stretch the word sound by sound, holding up 1 finger for each sound.)* **/eee/sss/**
(Teacher and students:) **/eee/sss/**

(Scaffold as necessary.)

Luego escribimos cada letra en el orden que la escuchamos. *(Demonstrate writing* es *on the marker board. Say the word as you write it.)*

Pasen a la página 34 en el *Libro de actividades* A. Miren los espacios para la actividad 2 en esta página.

Ahora, ustedes solos. Estiren es. **/eee/sss/**

(Scaffold as necessary.)

Escriban es en el primer espacio. Escriban cada letra en el orden en que la escuchan. *(Students should write* es.*)*

¿Qué palabra escribieron? es

Siguiente. *(Pause.)* **Se.**
Estiren se. **/sss/eee/**

(Scaffold as necessary.)

Escriban se en el siguiente espacio.
Escriban cada letra en el orden en que la escuchan. *(Students should write* se.*)*

(Monitor that each student writes the letters in the correct order. Correct as necessary.)

¿Qué palabra escribieron? se

Repeat the process with the following words: ese, sal, sala, sale, me, mes, mesa.

¡Buen trabajo estirando y escribiendo las palabras! Terminamos esta actividad. Marcaré la Hoja de maestría, y podemos pasar a la siguiente parte de nuestra lección.

Dejen el libro de actividades abierto porque lo usaremos más tarde.

162 Lesson 20

Nombre

Lección 20

Actividad 1

d	e	n	p
A	L	m	N
P	E	s	l

Actividad 2

es	se	ese
sal	sala	sale
me	mes	mesa

Libro de actividades A

Copyright © The McGraw-Hill Companies, Inc.

Nombre

Lección 20

Actividad 1

d	e	n	p
A	L	m	N
P	E	s	l

Actividad 2

es	se	ese
sal	sala	sale
me	mes	mesa

Libro de actividades A

Copyright © The McGraw-Hill Companies, Inc.

Nombre

Lección 20

Actividad 1

d	e	n	p
A	L	m	N
P	E	s	l

Actividad 2

es	se	ese
sal	sala	sale
me	mes	mesa

Word Recognition and Spelling (Teacher's Edition A): Writing the Sentence

The Stretch and Spell activities students have been practicing are preparing them for writing and spelling words in a sentence. In this activity, students write the words in a sentence as the words are dictated by the teacher. Scaffold the activity by asking students to write the sounds in the sequence in which they hear them in the word. Students write the sentence in their activity books.

ACTIVITY AT A GLANCE

- Step 1: Use the marker board to scaffold when students have difficulty writing a punctuation mark or a word used in the sentence.

- Step 2: Tell students to listen as you say the sentence: **¿Deseas nadar en el lago? (Would you like to swim in the lake?)** Repeat the sentence.

- Step 3: Demonstrate on the marker board how to write a punctuation mark. Explain: **Cuando escribimos una pregunta, ponemos un signo de interrogación al principio y otro al final. (When writing a question, we write a question mark at the beginning and at the end of the sentence.)**

- Step 4: Dictate the first word of the sentence: **Escriban *Deseas*. Escriban la palabra siguiendo el orden de los sonidos de las letras. (Write "deseas" in the order you hear the sounds.)**

- Step 5: Repeat the process for the remaining words in the sentence.

- Step 6: End with individual mastery check by monitoring to make sure that students have accurately written the words.

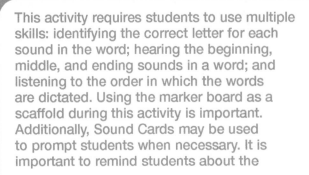

IN THE REAL WORLD

This activity requires students to use multiple skills: identifying the correct letter for each sound in the word; hearing the beginning, middle, and ending sounds in a word; and listening to the order in which the words are dictated. Using the marker board as a scaffold during this activity is important. Additionally, Sound Cards may be used to prompt students when necessary. It is important to remind students about the appropriate use of punctuation marks. For example, when a question mark is required, explain: **La oración es una pregunta. Escriban el signo de interrogación al principio y otro al final. (This sentence is a question, so write the question mark at the beginning and at the end.)** Also remind students that the first word in a sentence begins with a capital letter.

Questions and Answers

Lesson 39

Activity 5
Writing the Sentence

(You will use the marker board for this activity.)

Miren el espacio para la actividad 5 en el *Libro de actividades A.*

Prepárense para escribir. Van a escribir una oración. Escúchenla. ¿*Deseas nadar en el lago?*

Escuchen otra vez. ¿*Deseas nadar en el lago?*

Digan la oración conmigo. *(Teacher and students:)* **¿***Deseas nadar en el lago?*

Pongan el dedo en el primer signo de la oración en el libro de actividades. Este es un signo de interrogación. Cuando escribimos una pregunta, ponemos un signo de interrogación al principio y otro al final.

Escriban *Deseas.* **Escriban la palabra siguiendo el orden de los sonidos de las letras.** *(Monitor to ensure the students are writing the sounds in the correct order.)*

¿Con qué tipo de letra debe comenzar una oración? *(Monitor.)* **Con mayúscula.**

Escriban la primera letra de *Deseas* **con mayúscula.**

Siguiente palabra.

> **Repeat the process with the following words: nadar, en, el, lago.**

La oración es una pregunta. Entonces, escriban el signo de interrogación al final.

Note: Some students may need help writing the punctuation mark. Demonstrate writing on the marker board.

Escuchen cómo leo la oración interrogativa. ¿*Deseas nadar en el lago?* **Ahora lean la oración interrogativa. ¿***Deseas nadar en el lago?*

¡Buen trabajo! Marcaré la Hoja de maestría, y podemos pasar a la siguiente parte de nuestra lección.

Word Recognition and Spelling (Teacher's Edition A): Multisyllabic Chunking

Chunking is a process that is used for reading multisyllabic words. Multisyllabic chunking occurs much sooner in Spanish than in English. As with all the strategies the students learn, it gradually changes over time as the students master the skills involved. When chunking is first introduced, the students are asked to read each word part or syllable before reading a word composed of two syllables. It is first presented in **Teacher's Edition A.** Initially, these activities are led by the teacher with scaffolding until students have mastered the process (Lesson 23, Activity 7). Later, these activities are led by the student.

ACTIVITY AT A GLANCE

- Step 1: Hold up the **Teacher's Edition** with the word list.
- Step 2: Scaffold by reading the first syllable as you slide your finger under *ma.*
- Step 3: Read the next syllable as you slide your finger under *pa.*
- Step 4: Read the word.
- Step 5: Read the word fast.
- Step 6: Now have students read the first syllable with you as you slide your finger under *ma.*
- Step 7: Have students read the next syllable with you as you slide your finger under *pa.*
- Step 8: Everyone reads the word and then reads the word again fast.
- Step 9: Repeat the process for the remaining words.
- Step 10: End with individual mastery check by having students read one or two words each.

Activity 4

Sounding Out

Chunking—Teacher Led

Note: In this activity the object is for students to read words by chunking them into syllables, and then reading the word fast. Stretching the sounds will be used to help scaffold.

Ahora vamos a formar palabras con las sílabas. Las palabras se forman de una o más sílabas.

Mi turno.

Leo la palabra sílaba por sílaba. Escuchen.

Leo la sílaba. (*Hold up the book so all students can see the words. Slide your finger under ma.*) *Ma.*

Leo la sílaba. (*Slide your finger under pa.*) *Pa.*

La leo rápidamente. (*Quickly slide your finger under the entire word.*) *Mapa.*

Háganlo conmigo. Leamos la sílaba. (*Slide your finger under ma.*)

(*Teacher and students:*) ma

Leamos la sílaba. (*Slide your finger under pa.*)

(*Teacher and students:*) pa

Leámosla rápidamente. (*Quickly slide your finger under the entire word.*)

(*Teacher and students:*) mapa

(*Scaffold as necessary.*)

Ustedes solos. Lean la sílaba. (*Slide your finger under ma.*) ma

Lean la sílaba. (*Slide your finger under pa.*) pa

Léanla rápidamente. (*Quickly slide your finger under the entire word.*) mapa

¡Muy bien!

Siguiente palabra.

> Repeat the process with the following words: **sala, mala, Lala.**

(*Scaffold as necessary.*)

Individual Practice

(*Provide individual practice with 1 word per student.*)

¡Buen trabajo! Completaron esta actividad correctamente. Marcaré la Hoja de maestría, y podemos pasar a la siguiente parte de nuestra lección.

mapa

sala

mala

Lala

Activity 7
Sounding Out
Chunking—Teacher Led

**Vamos a leer palabras multisilábicas.
Primero piensen en los sonidos de las
sílabas y léanlas cuando las señale. Luego
lean la palabra rápidamente.**

*(Hold up the book so all students can see the
words.)*

Piensen. *(Touch under each letter in so.)*
Lean la sílaba. *(Slide your finger under so.)* **so**
Piensen. *(Touch under each letter in lar.)*
Lean la sílaba. *(Slide your finger under lar.)* **lar**
Lean la palabra rápidamente. *(Quickly slide
your finger under the entire word.)* **solar**
(Monitor and scaffold as necessary.)

Siguiente palabra.

> **Repeat the process with the following
> words: donde, salsa, pelón, damas,
> *espalda.**

Note: * Introduce the word as practice, but do
not require students to master it.

> **Repeat the process with the remaining
> words.**

Individual Practice

*(Provide individual practice with 2 or 3 words per
student.)*

**¡Buen trabajo leyendo las palabras!
Marcaré esta actividad en la Hoja de
maestría.**

pelón
damas
espalda

solar
donde
salsa

Word Recognition and Spelling (Teacher's Edition B)

The activities covered in the Word Recognition and Spelling Strand in **Teacher's Edition B** come from the same categories of skills taught in **Teacher's Edition A:** Sounding Out, Reading Fast First, High-Frequency Words, Stretch and Spell, Writing Sentences, Multisyllabic Chunking, and What Syllable Now? However, the What Syllable Now? Game appears only a few times, with greater emphasis on the new activity, What Word Now? Because the instructional process for the activities in **Teacher's Edition B** is the same as the procedures in **Teacher's Edition A,** students focus on reading longer words, (for example, four-syllable words), writing more sentences (two), and sounding out with greater independence (student-led). The instructional emphasis in **Teacher's Edition B** is increasingly on developing fluency and reading comprehension skills. Only the examples of the following activities will be in included in this section: What Word Now? Game and Sounding Out Chunking (Student Led).

What Word Now?

The purpose of the What Word Now? activity is to teach students that the omission or addition of even one sound can effectively change the way a word is read as well as the word's meaning. In this activity, you write a word on the board. Students read the word. You then change the word by adding or removing only one letter.

ACTIVITY AT A GLANCE

- Step 1: Write a word on the marker board.
- Step 2: Have students read the word.
- Step 3: Change the word by adding or removing one sound.
- Step 4: Students read the new word.
- Step 5: Repeat the procedure for the remaining words.
- Step 6: Provide individual practice with one or two words per student.

IN THE REAL WORLD

In this activity, students have the opportunity to learn how the omission or addition of a written accent changes the meaning of the word in Spanish. For example, in Lesson 47, Activity 7, students read **papas (potatoes)** and **papá (father).** This is a good time to point out other similar words in the Spanish language in which the omission or addition of an accented syllable changes the meaning of the word.

Questions and Answers

Activity 7
What Word Now? Game

(You will use the marker board for this activity.)

(Write the word papas on the marker board.)

Vamos a jugar a un juego que se llama "¿Qué palabra es ahora?".

Cuando señale una palabra, léanla. Luego voy a borrar una letra de la palabra y agregaré otra letra. Van a leer la palabra nueva.

Vamos a jugar.

Lean la palabra. papas

Ahora borro la s y agrego un acento en la segunda a. *(Erase the s and add accent on the last a. Slide your finger under the new word.)*

Lean la palabra nueva. papá

¡Muy bien!

(Scaffold as necessary.)

Ahora borro la segunda p en papá y añado la letra t. Borro el acento de la segunda a. *(Erase the last p and write t in its place. Erase the accent.)*

Lean la palabra nueva. pata

> **Repeat the process to create the following words: patos, gatos, gato, gata, lata, pata, pato.**

(Scaffold as necessary.)

Individual Practice

(Provide individual practice. Go through the list backwards.)

¡Buen trabajo! Puedo marcar la caja para esta actividad en la Hoja de maestría.

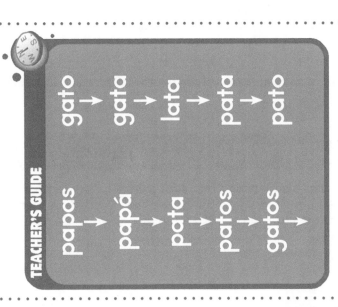

TEACHER'S GUIDE

papas → gato

papá → gata

pata → lata

patos → pata

gatos → pato

Multisyllabic Chunking

This procedure is the same for this activity as presented in **Teacher's Edition A.** However, instead of the teacher guiding the students to chunk words by syllables before reading the word, this activity is now student led.

ACTIVITY AT A GLANCE

- Step 1: Students slide their fingers under the first syllable and read the syllable.
- Step 2: Students slide their fingers under the second syllable and read the syllable.
- Step 3: Students slide their fingers under the third syllable and read the syllable.

- Step 4: Have students read the word fast.
- Step 5: Repeat the process for the remaining words.
- Step 6: Provide individual practice with one or two words per student.

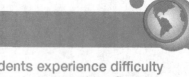

IN THE REAL WORLD

Once students understand that a long word (more than three syllables) can be broken down into manageable chunks that can be sounded out, they are more comfortable reading multisyllabic words.

Sometimes students experience difficulty when reading the parts together. Control their reading pace by telling students to read the part when they touch under the part, and then to read the next part only when they touch under it. Pick up the pace as the students get more comfortable with reading the parts.

Questions and Answers

Lesson 66

Activity 7
Sounding Out
Chunking—Student Led

Pasen a la página 54 en el *Libro de actividades B.*

Ahora van a formar palabras multisilábicas. Van a leer cada palabra por sílabas y luego la van a leer rápidamente. Pongan el dedo en la primera palabra.

Lean la sílaba. (*Students should slide a finger under mu.*) mu

Lean la sílaba. (*Students should slide a finger under ñe.*) ñe

Lean la sílaba. (*Students should slide a finger under ca.*) ca

Léan la palabra rápidamente. (*Students should quickly slide a finger under the entire word.*) muñeca

¡Muy bien!

Siguiente palabra.

> **Repeat the process with the following words: hermana, visitar, rosada, padres, regalo, hermosa, también.**

(*Scaffold as necessary.*)

Individual Practice
(*Provide individual practice.*)

¡Buen trabajo leyendo las palabras! Marcaré esta actividad en la Hoja de maestría, y pasaremos a la siguiente actividad.

Dejen el libro de actividades abierto porque lo usaremos más tarde.

Word Recognition and Spelling (Teacher's Edition C)

The activities covered in the Word Recognition and Spelling strand in **Teacher's Edition C** come from the same categories of skills taught in **Teacher's Editions A** and **B** and are taught mostly using the same procedures. Most instruction in **Teacher's Edition C** focuses on developing fluency and reading comprehension skills. However, an example is provided for the Reading Syllables task, as students now read longer lists of syllables that appear in the **Teacher's Edition** and not on Syllable Cards. These syllables often contain vowel diphthongs or consonant blends.

Reading Syllables

In this activity, students read syllables that begin with the consonant blends: *dr, pr, tr, fr,* and *gr.* Instead of using the Syllable Cards, use **Teacher's Edition C** and the same procedure for reviewing letter-sound correspondences. Students read the syllables fast.

ACTIVITY AT A GLANCE

- Step 1: Touch under the first syllable and say, **Lean la sílaba. (Read the syllable.)**
- Step 2: Repeat the process for the remaining syllables.
- Step 3: End with individual mastery check by having each student read two rows of syllables.

IN THE REAL WORLD

In this activity, it is important that students are able to read the syllables fast and do not separate syllables into individual sounds.

Questions and Answers

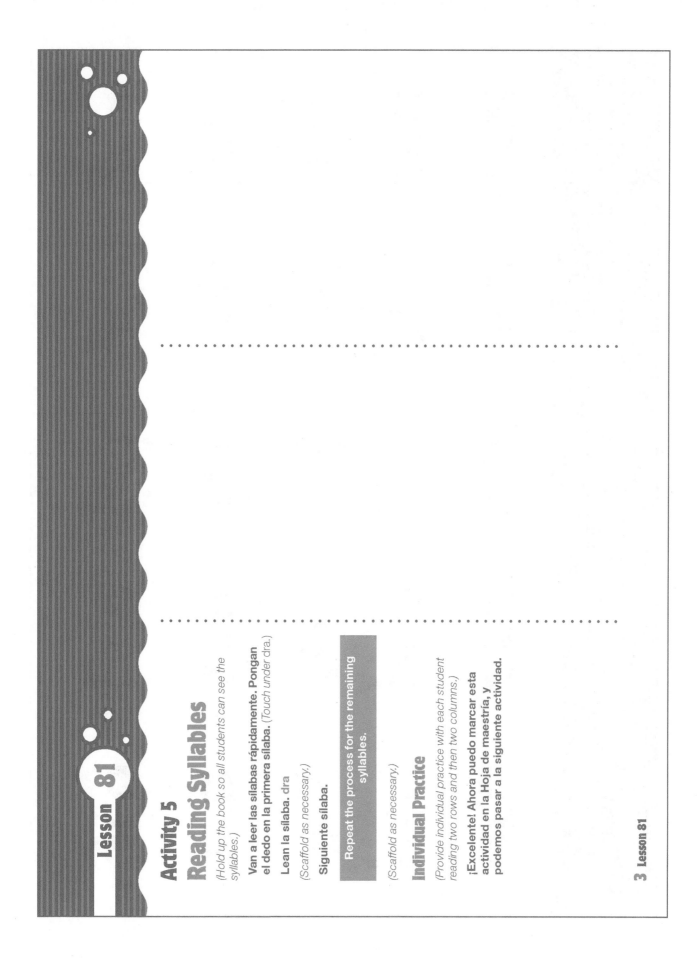

Lesson 81

Activity 5
Reading Syllables

(Hold up the book so all students can see the syllables.)

Van a leer las sílabas rápidamente. Pongan el dedo en la primera sílaba. *(Touch under dra.)*

Lean la sílaba. dra

(Scaffold as necessary.)

Siguiente sílaba.

Repeat the process for the remaining syllables.

(Scaffold as necessary.)

Individual Practice

(Provide individual practice with each student reading two rows and then two columns.)

¡Excelente! Ahora puedo marcar esta actividad en la Hoja de maestría, y podemos pasar a la siguiente actividad.

3 Lesson 81

dra   dre   dri   dro   dru

pra   pre   pri   pro   pru

tra   tre   tri   tro   tru

fra   fre   fri   fro   fru

gra   gre   gri   gro   gru

Strand Four: Fluency

The Fluency Strand is designed to build reading fluency. When a reader is fluent, she or he is able to decode text accurately and automatically. Two components of fluency are accuracy and speed. Accuracy is the fluent reading of unknown words and the immediate recognition of previously encountered words. Speed is the smoothness with which an individual reads connected text.

Fluency directly impacts comprehension. Students who struggle to read tend to have weak comprehension skills. In the Fluency Strand, students are provided with plenty of opportunities to read text that is familiar, predictable, and decodable in order to develop fluency.

Fluency is measured as words per minute (wpm). Once students are reading all the words in a story "fast first," begin to monitor fluency by timing readings. (Timed readings begin in Lesson 29.) When monitoring begins, students are initially expected to be reading only about 20 wpm. Over time, the fluency goal increases about 2 wpm per week. At the same time the text becomes more difficult. By the end of the intervention materials, students attain normal grade-level fluency.

Once fluency monitoring begins, a fluency goal is provided for each story. If students meet these goals for the stories, they are well on their way to becoming fluent readers. Preview each story-reading activity before working with students so that you know is expected of them.

Fluency (Teacher's Editions A, B, C): Reading Connected Text

Reading progresses through several phases in the Fluency Strand. Students begin reading connected text by sounding out and reading fast one to five sentences from the **Teacher's Edition.** Once students are reading text on their own, the **Libros decodificables (Decodable Books)** are introduced.

Fluency (Teacher's Edition A): Reading Simple Text

Simple Text—Teacher Led

The Fluency strand starts with simple text presented using the **Teacher's Edition.** To teach this format, hold the **Teacher's Edition** so all students can see the text. Use your finger for a visual guide for students to follow in order to read in unison. Students decode simple text sound by sound. For each decodable word say, **Digan los sonidos (Say the sounds),** moving your finger under each letter. For each high-frequency word say, **Léanla (Read it),** as you tap quickly under the word. After students sound out the sentence, say, **Léanla rápidamente (Read it fast).**

In the first few lessons, there are directional arrows and dots underneath the words as another visual cue for students. The arrows and dots gradually fade from the simple text prior to reading the **Decodable Books.** Reading simple text remains a teacher-led, sounding out, and reading fast activity.

ACTIVITY AT A GLANCE

- Step 1: Hold up the story in **Teacher's Edition** so students can see the story.
- Step 2: For each decodable word say **Digan los sonidos (Say the sounds)**, moving your finger under each letter. For each high-frequency word say, **Léanla (Read the word)**, as you tap quickly under the word.

- Step 3: After the students have sounded out the sentence, they read it the fast way. Say **Léanla rápidamente (Read it fast)** as you slide your finger under each decodable word, and touch quickly under high-frequency words.
- Step 4: Repeat the procedure with the remaining sentences.
- Step 5: End with individual practice of one sentence per student. Do not tap during individual practice.

IN THE REAL WORLD

Take the time to train your students to read a word only on your tap. If they are not reading together, stop them, repeat your instruction to read only when you tap, and start again. Unison reading allows you to monitor all your students at the same time and gives optimal reading time to each student.

Students read sentences until they can read smoothly.

When students are sounding out a word, touch under each letter, holding continuous sounds and moving off stop sounds quickly.

If students make an error as they read a sentence, have them sound out the word and read it fast. Then have then go back to the beginning of the sentence and begin again.

If students are making a lot of errors, slow the pace a bit. Once they are able to read the words smoothly, you can have them read the sentence faster.

Questions and Answers

Staff Development Guide, Spanish

Lesson 10

Activity 7
Connected Text
Fluency Development

Note: Use the following format: Tap under each high-frequency word; however, for each decodable word, slide your finger along the arrow under each letter. Sound out the word, and then read it fast. Then use the same process when students read the sentence. Finally, students read the sentence fast. If students hesitate, use the following cues: "Léanla" for high-frequency words (palabras de uso frecuente), then "Digan los sonidos" for decodable words, and "Léanla rápidamente" after students sound out the sentence. Always have students read the sentence fast after they sound out the words in the sentence.

Vamos a leer una oración. Mi turno.
(Demonstrate reading the sentence. Hold up the book so all students can see the sentences. Slide your finger under each letter in Mamá as you sound it out.) **/MMM/aaa/mmm/aaa/ Mamá.** *(Tap under me and read the word.)* **Me.** *(Slide your finger under each letter in a ama as you sound it out.)* **/aaa/mmm/aaa/ ama. /MMM/aaa/mmm/aaa Mamá me /aaa/mmm/aaa/ ama.**

(Read the sentence as you tap under each word. Read slowly, and then again at normal speed.)

Mamá me ama. *(Pause.)* **Mamá me ama.**

80 Lesson 10

Ahora vamos a leerla juntos. Cuando señale una palabra de uso frecuente, la leeremos rápidamente. Las demás palabras las diremos sonido por sonido y después las leeremos rápidamente. *(Cue students by sliding your finger under each letter in Mamá as you sound it out with students. Tap under the frequent word, me. Slide your finger under each letter in ama as you sound it out with students. Scaffold as necessary.)*

(Teacher and students:)
/MMM/aaa/mmm/aaa/ Mamá me /aaa/mmm/aaa/ ama.

Léanla conmigo lentamente.
(Teacher and students:) **Mamá me ama.** *(Pause.)*

Léanla rápidamente conmigo.
(Teacher and students:) **Mamá me ama.**

Ustedes solos. /MMM/aaa/mmm/aaa/ Mamá me /aaa/mmm/aaa/ ama. *(Slide your finger under each letter in mamá. Tap under the high-frequency word, me. Slide your finger under each letter in ama.)*

Léanla lentamente. Mamá me ama. *(Pause.)*
Léanla rápidamente. Mamá me ama.

Siguiente.

> **Repeat the process for the following sentences: Mi mamá me ama. ¿Me amas?**

Individual Practice
(Provide individual practice.)

(Point out punctuation marks at the end of sentences and question marks in ¿Me amas?.)

Las primeras dos oraciones son declaraciones y terminan con un punto. La última oración empieza y termina con un signo de interrogación. Es una pregunta.

¡Muy bien! Completaron esta actividad perfectamente. Marcaré la última actividad en la Hoja de maestría para esta lección, y como han terminado esta lección, puedo poner un adhesivo en la Hoja de maestría.

Staff Development Guide, Spanish

111

Mamá me ama.

Mi mamá me ama.

¿Me amas?

Reading Decodable Books

The **Decodable Books** are fully decodable, meaning that all the words are composed of only previously taught letter-sound elements or high-frequency words. Initially students are taught to read high-frequency words fast but to sound out decodable words sound by sound. For this format, softly tap once for each sound, and then tell students, **Léanla (Read it).** Tap once for each high-frequency word.

Soon students sound out syllables by phonemes before blending the syllables into words. The sounding-out process then quickly changes to sounding out words by chunking them into syllables and then reading the words fast.

After students have sounded out and read each word in the sentence, they go back and read the sentence the fast way, following your auditory cue.

ACTIVITY AT A GLANCE

- Step 1: Review or preteach selected story words.
- Step 2: Students browse the story and make a prediction.
- Step 3: Students read the title of the story in unison.
- Step 4: Review the sounding-out process used in the story prior to reading. When sounding out words sound by sound, tap once for each high-frequency word, once for each sound in a decodable word, and then once to read that word. When reading syllables sound by sound, tap once for each sound in the syllable and once to read the syllable. Do this for each syllable, and then tap and ask, **¿Qué palabra? (What word?)** When chunking words by syllables, tap once for each syllable, allowing enough time between taps for students to read syllables from decodable words. Then have students read the word fast. The maximum think time per word is specified in each reading activity.
- Step 5: After sounding out a sentence, students read the sentence fast.

- Step 6: Repeat the procedure with the remaining sentences on each page.
- Step 7: Students review any words they missed as they read the story. Write all the missed words on the marker board. Have students sound out each word to themselves and then read the word fast. Then have the students read the list of missed words the fast way.
- Step 8: Discuss predictions with students.
- Step 9: Have students read the story a second time. This time they read the story fast, sounding out the words to themselves. Tap once for each word, allowing enough time between taps for students to sound out the decodable words to themselves. Start the timer with the first tap.
- Step 10: If a fluency goal is provided, start the timer, and have students read the book, taking turns reading one or two pages at a time for individual practice. Stop the timer when students have completed reading the entire book.
- Step 11: Review missed words.

If students are consistently struggling to meet their fluency goal, you need to assess the problem. Have they met mastery on the list of missed words before they read the story again? Do you need to slow the pace by allowing more think time between taps?

Questions and Answers

Lesson 14

Activity 8
Decodable Book

Part A: Review High-Frequency Words

(Have ready Tarjetas de palabras de uso frecuente—esta, es, me.)

Vamos a repasar algunas palabras de uso frecuente. *(Hold up* esta.*)* **Esta palabra es** *esta.* **Léanla.** esta

(Hold up es.*)* **¿Cuál es esta palabra?** es
(Hold up me.*)* **¿Cuál es esta palabra?** me

(Shuffle and repeat.)

Individual Practice

(Provide individual practice.)

Part B: Fluency Development

(Pass out **Libro decodificable 1,** Lala, *to students. Hold up your book so students can see the front of the book.)*

Ahora vamos a leer nuestro cuento. Cuando saquen el libro, pongan el dedo en el título del cuento.

(Point to the title, Lala, *on page 1.)* **El título de este cuento es** *Lala.* **¿Cuál es el título?** Lala

(Browse the story. Page through the story with students, asking them to comment on what they see. Ask them what they think the story will be about.) **Vamos a mirar los dibujos. Abran el libro y miren todos los dibujos del cuento. Vamos a hacer esto rápidamente antes de leer. ¿Tienen alguna idea de qué trata el cuento?** *(Discuss students' predictions. Possible student response:* El cuento es sobre Lala y una chica.*)* **Vamos a leer y ver.**

Note: Follow this format: Tap under each high-frequency word. For each decodable word, slide your finger under each letter. Sound out the word and then read it fast. Then use the same process when students read the sentence. Finally, students read the sentence fast. If students hesitate, use the following cues: "Léanla" for high-frequency words (palabras frecuentes), then "Digan los sonidos" for decodable words, and "Léanla rápidamente" after students sound out the sentence. Students should follow along with their finger, touching under each word as they read it fast.

Este cuento tiene muchas oraciones. Vamos a leer esas oraciones. Ustedes saben cómo leerlas. Cuando lean la primera vez, lean las palabras frecuentes rápidamente. Las demás palabras, léanlas sonido por sonido y después rápidamente. Cuando vayan a leer la segunda vez, daré un golpecito para cada palabra. Cuando oigan ese golpecito, lean la palabra rápidamente. Ahora, abran el libro.

(Demonstrate reading as students follow along.)

Mi turno. Yo leeré primero. Esta oración tiene palabras frecuentes. Cuando las señale, las leeré rápidamente.

(Tap.) **Esta** *(tap)* **es** /LLL/aaa/lll/aaa/ **Lala.** **Leo la oración.** *(Tap.)* **Esta** *(tap)* **es** *(tap)* **Lala.**

Vamos a decir los sonidos de las palabras. Háganlo conmigo. Listos. *(As you move your finger under the word, have students sound out all words except for high-frequency words. Scaffold as necessary, and then have students read the sentence.)*
(Teacher and students:) (Tap.) **Esta** *(tap)* **es** /LLL/aaa/lll/aaa/ **Lala.**

(Scaffold as necessary.)

Lean conmigo. *(Teacher and students:) (Tap.)* **Esta** *(tap)* **es** *(tap)* **Lala.**

Siguiente página. Pongan el dedo en la primera palabra. Digan los sonidos conmigo. *(Pause.) (Slide your finger under the decodable words as they are sounded out, then read them at normal speed. Tap under the high-frequency word, me as it is read.)*
(Teacher and students:)
/Lll/aaa/lll/aaa/ **Lala** *(tap)* **me** /aaa/mmm/aaa/ **ama.**

(Scaffold as necessary.)

Lean conmigo. *(Teacher and students:) (Tap.)* **Lala** *(tap)* **me** *(tap)* **ama.**

Siguiente página. Listos. Pongan el dedo en la primera palabra. Digan los sonidos conmigo. *(Pause.) (Tap under the high-frequency word, me as it is read. Slide your finger under the decodable words as they are sounded out, then read them at normal speed.)*
(Teacher and students:) (Tap.) **Me** /aaa/mmm/aaa/ **ama** /Lll/aaa/lll/aaa/ **Lala.**

(Scaffold as necessary.)

120 Lesson 14

Lean conmigo. *(Teacher and students:) (Tap.)* **Me** *(tap)* **ama** *(tap)* **Lala.**

Ahora lean conmigo todas las oraciones. *(Pause.)* **Regresen a la página 4. Listos.**

(Teacher and students:)
(Tap.) **Esta** *(tap)* **es** *(tap)* **Lala.**
(Tap.) **Lala** *(tap)* **me** *(tap)* **ama.**
(Tap.) **Me** *(tap)* **ama** *(tap)* **Lala.**

(Scaffold as necessary.)

Ustedes solos. Lean las oraciones. Listos. Pongan el dedo en la primera palabra.

(Tap.) **Esta** *(tap)* **es** *(tap)* **Lala.**
(Tap.) **Lala** *(tap)* **me** *(tap)* **ama.**
(Tap.) **Me** *(tap)* **ama** *(tap)* **Lala.**

(Scaffold as necessary.)

¡Buen trabajo leyendo las oraciones!

(If a student makes a mistake, use the following procedure.)

ERROR CORRECTION:
Vamos a ver esa palabra. *(Have students look at the word.)*
La palabra es _____. *(Read the word.)*
¿Qué palabra? *(Touch under the word. Students should read the word.)*
Muy bien. Ahora vamos a empezar desde el principio de la oración.

Individual Practice

(Provide individual practice with 1 sentence per student.)

(Discuss predictions.) **¿Se realizó nuestra predicción? ¿El cuento era sobre Lala y una chica?**
(Ask students:) **¿Quién ama a la chica?** Lala

¡Muy bien! Completaron esta actividad perfectamente. Hemos terminado todas las partes de nuestra lección. Eso significa que puedo poner un adhesivo en la Hoja de maestría de esta lección.

Activity 10
Decodable Book
Fluency Development

(Pass out *Libro decodificable 5*, Pepe y las papas, to students. Have the marker board ready.)

Note: Follow this format: Have students read from their own books, touching under each word as they read it. Tap once for each high-frequency word. For decodable words, tap once for each syllable, allowing enough time between taps for students to read syllables from decodable words. Then have students read the word fast. Finally, students read the sentence fast. Allow no more than 2 seconds think time per word sounds in decoding.

If students hesitate, use the following cues: "Léanla" for high-frequency words (palabras frecuentes); "Lean las sílabas" for decodable words, and "Léanla rápidamente" after students sound out the sentence. Always have students read the sentence fast after they sound out the words. Use taps and verbal cues as necessary to set the pace and to keep students reading together.

Van a hojear el libro y mirar los dibujos.
¿Qué piensan que va a pasar en el cuento?
(Accept reasonable responses, and then have students make 1 prediction about the story.)

Van a leer el cuento *Pepe y las papas.*
Leamos el título juntos.
Pongan el dedo en la primera palabra.
(Monitor.
(You may have to physically place students' fingers on the first word to follow.)

Listos. *(Pause.)*
(Teacher and students:) (Tap.) **Pe** *(tap)* **pe**
¿Qué palabra? Pepe
(Tap.) **y**
(Tap.) **las**
(Tap.) **pa** *(tap)* **pas**
¿Qué palabra? papas

¿Cuál es el título?
(Teacher and students:) (Tap.) **Pepe** *(tap)* **y** *(tap)*
las *(tap)* **papas**

(Scaffold as necessary.)

184 Lesson 22

Lesson 22

Ahora van a leer ustedes solos. Miren la página 3. Listos.
(Tap.) **Pe** *(tap)* **pe**
¿Qué palabra? Pepe
(Tap.) **de** *(tap)* **se** *(tap)* **a**
¿Qué palabra? desea
(Tap.) **las**
¿Qué palabra? las
(Tap.) **pa** *(tap)* **pas**
¿Qué palabra? papas
(Tap.) **sa** *(tap)* **la** *(tap)* **das**
¿Qué palabra? saladas.

> **Repeat the format with the rest of the story.**

Note: If any errors occur, record the words missed on the marker board for later review. Have students sound out the word by syllables as a group. If they continue to miss words, sound each syllable, and then have them read the word fast. Finally, ask them to read the word fast.

¿Qué pasó en el cuento? ¿Se cumplió lo que ustedes pensaron que iba a ocurrir?
(Accept reasonable responses.)

Individual Practice

(Provide individual practice, with each student reading one page.)

Ahora van a leer rápidamente. Listos.
(Tap.) **Pepe** *(tap)* **desea** *(tap)* **las** *(tap)* **papas** *(tap)* **saladas.**

> **Repeat the process with the remaining sentences.**

¡Buen trabajo! Completaron esta actividad perfectamente. Marcaré la última actividad en la Hoja de maestría y puedo poner un adhesivo en la Hoja de maestría de esta lección.

Fluency
(Teacher's Editions A, B, C): Decodable Books

Decodable Books: Reading Fast First

Once students are reading stories by reading words fast first, story reading takes on a predictable set of steps. Building on research about the importance of repeated readings, each story is read multiple times. The objective is to read with increasing fluency on each subsequent reading.

ACTIVITY AT A GLANCE

- Step 1: Review or preteach selected story words.
- Step 2: Students browse the story and make a prediction.
- Step 3: Students read the title of the story in unison.
- Step 4: Students read the story as you tap softly on the table once for each word. The maximum think time per word is specified in each reading activity. Start the timer with the first tap, and time the reading.

- Step 5: Discuss predictions with students.
- Step 6: Review missed words.
- Step 7: If students meet fluency goal, move to Individual Practice. If the fluency goal is not met, students read the story in unison a second time. This time students read faster. After the second unison reading, complete Individual Practice. Time the Individual Practice and record on the Mastery Sheet whether the group met the fluency goal.
- Step 8: Review missed words.

IN THE REAL WORLD

If an error occurs, have the students sound out the word together in a whisper voice, read the word fast, and then go back and reread the sentence.

Questions and Answers

Lesson 31

Activity 8
Decodable Book
Fluency Development

(You will use the timer and the marker board for this activity.)

*(Pass out **Libro decodificable 7,** Los alaridos de Alí, to students.)*

FLUENCY GOAL 24 words @ 20 words per minute (wpm) = 1 minute, 20 seconds. For all fluency goals, 5–10 second have been added to the goal time to allow for switching students while reading.

Note: Use the following format: Have students read from their own books, touching under the words as they read them. Students read fast first the first time in unison. Tap once for each word, allowing enough think time between taps for students to sound out decodable words in their heads.

Ahora vamos a leer el cuento *Los alaridos de Alí.* **Si saben la palabra, díganla cuando dé un golpecito. Si no saben la palabra, díganla por sílabas en silencio, y luego díganla rápidamente en voz alta cuando yo dé un golpecito. Les daré tiempo para pensar antes de que golpee. Pongan el dedo en cada palabra en su libro. Listos.** *(Monitor.)*

(Provide think time—3 seconds maximum per word, start timer, and tap.)

Repeat the process with the entire story.

Note: Follow the usual error correction process for reading activities. Use the marker board to review any missed words.

Individual Practice

(Call on individual students to read 1 or 2 pages. Monitor to be sure all students are following along. Do not tap during individual practice. Time group reading. Note on the Mastery Sheet whether the group achieved the fluency goal.)

¡Muy bien! Completaron esta actividad perfectamente. Marcaré esta actividad en la Hoja de maestría, y puedo poner un adhesivo en la Hoja de maestría de esta lección.

Use of Auditory Cues

The auditory cue during group reading is a tool for controlling think time. To help students meet the fluency goals, tap softly on the table for each word read. Pausing between taps sets the pace at which the students read. The pause provides think time, which allows students enough time to figure out the unknown words, while moving students through the text as fast as they can read without error. Taps must be predictable and consistent, like a metronome.

The amount of think time is listed within each reading activity, and the amount of time gradually decreases throughout the curriculum to support fluency development. Do not tap during individual practice. During individual practice, students read as fast as they can without making errors.

Story Reading Routine: Day 1

Students will usually read the same story for two days. The first day the group reads the story two or three times. First the group reads the story in unison. Control the pace by tapping softly to cue students to read the next word. Each lesson specifies the maximum allowable think time between taps if students are to achieve the fluency goal. However, if students can read faster than the specified rate, you may set a slightly faster pace.

Read the story in unison a second time only if the group struggled to meet the maximum allowable think time for each word and did not meet the fluency goal for the story on the first read. Also, if multiple errors occurred in the first reading, students should read the story again in unison. However, if the group easily met the fluency goal and made less than two errors as a group, you can skip the second reading and move directly to individual practice. Before rereading the story, write any missed words on the board, and have students sound out the words and read them fast. Repeat this process with each rereading of the story.

The second time the group reads the story in unison, push the group to read a little faster. Again control the pacing with soft taps.

During individual practice, each student reads one or two pages, while the other students follow along by pointing to each word with their fingers. Importantly, time how long it takes the group to read the story and then record on the Mastery Sheet whether the group met the fluency goal for the story.

Story Reading Routine: Day 2 (Teacher's Editions B and C)

On the second day of reading a story, students are expected to read the story with greater fluency than the day before. Time the group again, and record on the Mastery Sheet whether the group met the fluency goal. If the group reads the story within the specified time, move to the next activity. If students are struggling to meet the fluency goal, have them repeat the reading. However, before rereading you may choose to model sections of the text.

Partner Reading: Beat the Clock

In **Teacher's Editions B** and **C,** you conduct Partner Reading: Beat the Clock on the second day of reading a story.

For Partner Reading: Beat the Clock, you will partner with one student. Switch partners each session. Have the remaining students partner with the student sitting next to them. Listen to your partner student reading the story. Students who are partnered take turns reading one page at a time from the same **Decodable Book.**

When conducting Partner Reading: Beat the Clock, tell all the students what the fluency goal is, and set a timer or a stopwatch. Students then read as fast and accurately as they can in order to read the entire story before time runs out. Record on the Mastery Sheet whether the student you partnered with met the fluency goal for the story.

Achieving Reading Fluency Goals

As students meet the fluency goals, they should be reading smoothly, with expression, and without errors. If students are consistently unable to meet their goals, there are several strategies available to assist them. First, make sure students are truly mastering the list of missed words before they read the story the second time. If students continue to make errors while they read the story, they are having difficulty transferring words in isolation into story text. In this instance, review the missed words again. Have students practice reading these words within the story. Then have students practice reading the sentence containing the missed word until they can read it smoothly and fluently.

You may need to slow the pace a little. Once students are reading smoothly and without error, pick up the pace. If the students are still having trouble meeting the fluency goals, you may need to go back and reteach selected activities that led up to the story. It may be that the students did not retain a certain letter-sound correspondence, word concept, or decoding skill and need reteaching.

Strand Five: Comprehension Strategies

Comprehension Strategy instruction develops your students' ability to process text strategically, to organize concepts and information for retrieval, and to monitor their own understanding of the text. Comprehension activities are conducted primarily orally to take advantage of the students' receptive and expressive vocabularies. Occasionally you will be directed to write the students' responses on the board.

Before Reading

Browsing the story begins in **Teacher's Edition A** and continues through the entire curriculum. Before reading a story, students look at the pictures and briefly discuss what they think the story is about. Read the title with the students, and ask them to make predictions about the story. Then set as the purpose for reading as reading to see if their predictions come true.

Preteach any story words that might be difficult for students (requires teacher judgment). Students then read the story to see if their predictions come true.

During Reading

During reading, observe whether students are listening to what they are reading. This can often be evidenced by their use of contextual clues to self-correct. If you suspect students are not following the storyline, you may briefly check comprehension.

After Reading

After reading, check the students' predictions. This holds students responsible for the material they have just read. They read to see if what they thought was going to happen does indeed occur. If the predictions do not come true, students should be able to tell you what did happen.

Comprehension Strategies (Teacher's Edition A)

The **Decodable Book** activities begin in Lesson 14. Comprehension strategies are introduced as soon as students begin to read the **Decodable Books.** Students learn to retell the story and sequence events as a basic, routine approach to organizing the information in the stories they read.

After Reading: Sequencing Information

One of the first after-reading comprehension strategies taught in **SRA Intervenciones tempranas de la lectura** is Sequencing (Lesson 23). Sequencing information in a story provides a simple organizational structure from which students are able to access information for more advanced comprehension tasks.

In the beginning, students retell anything they remember from the story. After several lessons, students are required to retell the events from the story in the order that they occurred. Then, the students transition to identifying the *main* events of the story in proper sequence.

Story Retell and Sequencing

Students learn to retell the story in their own words, relating each event in the order that it happened. The overall retell should be brief, taking no more than one or two minutes.

ACTIVITY AT A GLANCE

- Step 1: After reading the story and reviewing missed words, have students retell the story in their own words, one event at a time, in the order the events occurred.
- Step 2: Prompt students: **¿Cómo comienza el cuento? (How does the story begin?)**
- Step 3: Prompt students: **¿Qué sucedió después? (What happened next?)**

- Step 4: Repeat the procedure until the story has been completely retold.
- Step 5: Individual mastery is achieved by calling on one student to retell what happened first, then calling on another student to say what happened next, and so on, until all students have identified at least one story event.

IN THE REAL WORLD

Answers may need to be scaffolded. Students may get the events out of order. They may relate an event incorrectly or bring in information that wasn't in the story. They may leave out events. If they get events out of order, prompt students by asking if the sequence makes sense. Prompt students by asking if one event may have occurred prior to another event. If they leave out events, have them browse through the book to see if they can self-correct. Finally, if they are really unable to retell the events, go back, reread the book one page at a time, and ask what is happening on each page. After the students answer, scaffold by asking them what happened next. Repeat the procedure with each remaining page.

Questions and Answers

Lesson 25

Activity 9
Decodable Book
Fluency Development

(Pass out Libro decodificable 6, El mono Noé, to students. Have the marker board ready.)

Note: Follow this format:

Have students read from their books, touching under each word as they read it. Teacher taps once for each high-frequency word and each syllable. Allow enough time between taps for students to read the syllables of decodable words. Then students read the word fast. Finally students read the sentence fast. If students hesitate, use the following cues: "Léanla" for high-frequency words, "Lean las sílabas" for decodable words, and "Léanla rápidamente" after students sound out the sentence. Use taps and oral cues as necessary. Allow no more than 2 seconds per syllable in decoding.

Van a repasar las palabras en las que se han equivocado en la lección anterior.

Note: Record missed words on the board that students missed from the previous lesson. Have students sound out the word by syllables as a group. If they continue to miss words, sound each syllable then have them read the word fast. Finally, ask them to read the word fast.

Van a leer el cuento *El mono Noé*. Leamos el título juntos.

(Teacher and students:) (Tap.) **El**
(Tap.) **mo** *(tap)* **no**
¿Qué palabra? **mono**
(Tap.) **No** *(tap)* **é**
¿Qué palabra? **Noé**
Leamos el título rápidamente. Listos.
(Pause.)
(Teacher and students:) (Tap.) **El** *(tap)* **mono** *(tap)* **Noé**

Voy a leer el cuento rápida y fluidamente. Mi turno. *(Read the whole story fluently.)*

Ahora ustedes van a leer el cuento rápidamente. Listos. *(Pause.)*

(Tap.) **¿Dónde** *(tap)* **está** *(tap)* **Nesa?** *(tap)* **No** *(tap)* **está** *(tap)* **en** *(tap)* **la** *(tap)* **sala.**

> Repeat the process with the remaining pages.

Individual Practice

(Have each student read one page of the story. Monitor students' fluency to make sure their reading is similar to that of yours.)

¡Muy buen trabajo leyendo el cuento rápida y fluidamente! Marcaré esta actividad en la Hoja de maestría.

Comprehension Strategies (Teacher's Edition B)

The activities covered in the Comprehension Strategies strand in **Teacher's Edition B** focus on the following comprehension strategies: Sequencing Main Events, Parts of a Story, What Do We Know?/What Did We Learn?, and Sentence Completion. These comprehension tasks focus the students on identifying the essential elements of the story: main characters, problem, main events, and outcome.

Comprehension Strategies (Teacher's Edition B): Sequencing Main Events

In **Teacher's Edition B** students are asked to identify only the *main* events of a story in proper sequence. Eventually this skill will support students when they are learning to summarize.

ACTIVITY AT A GLANCE

- Step 1: Students identify and sequence main events of the story.
- Step 2: Prompt students, **¿Qué pasa primero? (What happens first?)**
- Step 3: Prompt students, **¿Qué pasa después? (What happens next?)**
- Step 4: Repeat the procedure until all the main events have been listed in sequence.

- Step 5: Individual mastery is achieved by calling on one student to say what happened first, then calling on another student to say what happened next, and so on, until all students have identified at least one event.

IN THE REAL WORLD

Students may try to retell everything that happened in the story. Scaffold their understanding of the difference between main events and story details. You may need to use a real-life example. For instance, your students woke up this morning, they came to school, and then they will go home. These are the three main events of their day. In between, they do class work, eat lunch, and talk with their friends, but these are not the main events.

Questions and Answers

Lesson 58

Activity 2
Reading Comprehension
Sequencing

(You will use the marker board for this activity.)

Vamos a hacer un resumen del cuento *Me gusta, no me gusta*. Aprendimos que hay cosas que le gustan al niño y cosas que no le gustan.
Vamos a hacer una lista de lo que le gusta.

(Write student responses on the marker board under the head Me gusta.)

¿Qué le gusta primero en el cuento? el helado de fruta
¿Qué le gusta luego en el cuento? el olor de las rosas
¿Qué le gusta después? el mar y el río
¿Qué le gusta después? las lomas y los terrenos llanos
¿Qué le gusta después? el humo de la barbacoa

(Summarize the story for students from what you have written on the marker board.)
(Scaffold as necessary. Scaffold with pictures if necessary.)

Quiero que lean la lista de lo que le gusta al niño.

(Slide your finger under Me gusta *el helado de fruta on the marker board.)*

Lean. Me gusta el helado de fruta.

> **Repeat the process with the entire *Me gusta* list.**

Ahora vamos a hacer una lista de lo que no le gusta al niño. *(Write student responses on the marker board under the head* No me gusta.)

¿Qué no le gusta primero en el cuento? la gente mala
¿Qué no le gusta luego en el cuento? la música ruidosa
¿Qué no le gusta después? comer fruta verde
¿Qué no le gusta después? estar en filas largas

Quiero que lean la lista de lo que no le gusta al niño.

(Slide your finger under No me gusta *la gente mala on the marker board.)*

Lean. No me gusta la gente mala.

> **Repeat the process with the entire *No me gusta* list.**

Abran sus libros en la página 8. *(Pause and monitor.)*

Lean la página. *(Have students read page 8 together.)*

Al final del cuento leemos otra lista que nombra las personas y animales que al niño también le gustan.

¿A qué grupo pertenecen la mamá, el papá, el hermano, el perro y el gato? a la familia
(Scaffold as necessary.)

¡Excelente! Completaron esta actividad perfectamente. Marcaré esta actividad en la Hoja de maestría, y podemos pasar a la siguiente actividad.

110 **Lesson 58**

Comprehension Strategies (Teacher's Edition B): Story Grammar

Story Grammar organizes the major elements of a story into main character(s), problem, and main events. Story Grammar provides a framework for students to examine the connections between story elements, which leads to a deeper understanding of a story.

ACTIVITY AT A GLANCE

- Step 1: Write the following words in a column on the marker board: **Quién, Problema, Eventos: 1, 2, 3, 4,** and **Final (Who, Problem, Events, End).**

- Step 2: Guide the students through each part. **¿Sobre quién trata el cuento? (Who is the story about?)** Write the response in the column **Quién (Who).**

- Step 3: **¿Cuál es el problema con _____ ? (What is the problem with _____?)** Write the response in the column **Problema (Problem).**

- Step 4: Ask guiding questions until all the main events have been retold. **¿Qué pasa primero? ¿Qué pasa después? ¿Qué pasa después? (What happens first? And next? And then?)** Write the events in correct sequence.

- Step 5: **¿Qué pasa al final del cuento? (What happens at the end?)** Write the response in the column **Final (End).**

- Step 6: Individual mastery is achieved by giving each student an opportunity to identity at least one major story element.

IN THE REAL WORLD

Story grammar is a logical activity for students. They understand what you want from them. They may be challenged in identifying certain elements and might require scaffolding. Sometimes students want to identify every character in the story as the main character. If this occurs, explain that there may be several people mentioned in the story, but the story is not mainly about all of them. The story is usually is about one or two people.

Questions and Answers

Activity 2
Comprehension
Story Grammar

(Write the following words vertically on the marker board: Quién, Problema, Eventos: 1, 2, 3, 4, *and* Final.*)*

Vamos a hablar de lo que acabamos de leer. ¿Sobre quién trata el cuento? Tino y Toni

Voy a escribir *Tino y Toni* al lado de *Quién* porque el cuento trata sobre ellos.
(Write Tino y Toni *beside* Quién.*)*

¿Cuál es el problema con Tino y Toni? La gente los confunde.

¡Muy bien! Voy a escribir *La gente los confunde* al lado de *Problema.*

¿Qué pasa primero? *(Accept reasonable responses such as:* La cara de Tino es como la de Toni, son iguales*).*

¿Qué pasa después? *(Accept reasonable responses such as:* A los dos les gusta lo mismo, usar gafas y salir a nadar.*)*

¿Qué pasa después? *(Accept reasonable responses such as:* La gente los confunde.*)*

¿Qué pasa después? *(Accept reasonable responses such as:* Les da risa porque la gente los confunde.*)*

¿Qué pasa al final del cuento? La gente los confunde porque son gemelos.

Voy a escribir *La gente los confunde porque son gemelos* al lado de *Final*.
(Monitor, correct, and scaffold as necessary.)

¡Muy buen trabajo resumiendo el cuento! Ahora puedo marcar la caja para esta actividad en la Hoja de maestría.

Staff Development Guide, Spanish   **129**

Comprehension Strategies (Teacher's Edition B): What Do We Know?/What Did We Learn? (¿Qué sabemos?/¿Qué aprendimos?)

What Do We Know?/What Did We Learn? is an activity that requires you to make a chart to record student responses before and after reading a story: Column 1: **¿Qué sabemos? (What do we know?)** Column 2: **¿Qué aprendimos? (What did we learn?)** Discussing and recording what students already know about a topic prior to reading provides an organizational framework through which students can understand and more easily recall new information. Identifying new information they learned through reading deepens student understanding of a selection.

ACTIVITY AT A GLANCE

- Step 1: Write the topic at the top of the marker board (e.g., **Cocodrilos**).

- Step 2: Under the topic, draw a vertical line to divide the marker board into two columns. At the top of the left column, write **¿Qué sabemos? (What do we know?)** At the top of the right column, write **¿Qué aprendimos? (What did we learn?)**.

- Step 3: Ask students what they already know about the topic. Scaffolding may be necessary to elicit answers depending on the unfamiliarity of the topic. Scaffolding can include reading the title of the story and browsing the story page by page with the students to solicit important background information on the topic. Scaffolding can also include asking guiding questions: **¿Qué es un cocodrilo? ¿Dónde viven los cocodrilos? (What is a crocodile? Where do crocodiles live?)**.

- Step 4: Write the students' answers in the left column under **¿Qué sabemos? (What do we know?)** (Do not erase the information in this column. You will use this chart in the next lesson.)

- Step 5: Read the story.

- Step 6: Review the information written in the left column under **¿Qué sabemos? (What do we know?)**

- Step 7: Draw a circle around the things that are true and cross out the things that are not true.

- Step 8: Read each page of the story. Students report what they learned about the topic.

- Step 9: Summarize the information.

- Step 10: Individual mastery for comprehension is achieved by letting each student take a turn telling what he or she learned from a page in the story.

IN THE REAL WORLD

If your students are reluctant at first to provide information for **"¿Qué sabemos?"** **(What do we know?)** or if they are prone to giving random answers, prompt them with questions that relate the topic to their lives. For example, when reading the book **Isidro,** you might ask **¿Qué es un cocodrilo? ¿Dónde viven los cocodrilos? ¿Dónde han visto los cocodrilos? ¿Qué comen los cocodrilos? Vamos a leer el cuento *Isidro* y aprender sobre los cocodrilos. (What is a crocodile? Where do crocodiles live? Where have you seen crocodiles? What do crocodiles eat? Let's read the story *Isidro* and learn about crocodiles.)** Sometimes students may be very savvy about a particular topic, and you will have to limit the amount of information they give you. Limit each student to one or two answers. After reading the book, summarize what children already knew about the topic. Always validate what students bring to the lesson. This builds their confidence and supports future learning.

Questions and Answers

Activity 5

Decodable Book

Part A: Fluency Development

(You will use the marker board and timer for this activity.)

*(Pass out **Libro decodificable 35,** Isidro, to students. Have students browse the story and make predictions.)*

Isidro

FLUENCY GOAL 78 words @ 39 wpm = 2 minutes 5 seconds per word.

(Write ¿Qué sabemos? and ¿Qué aprendimos? on the marker board.)

(Read the title Isidro and browse the story page by page with the students to solicit background information on crocodiles—i.e. what the students know.)

¿Qué es un cocodrilo?
(Accept reasonable responses.)

¿Dónde viven los cocodrilos?
(Accept reasonable responses.)

¿Qué son los juncos?
(Accept reasonable responses.)
(Write information gathered from the students under ¿Qué sabemos? on the marker board.)

Vamos a leer un cuento sobre un cocodrilo.

Note: Provide no more than 2 seconds maximum think time per word.

Ahora leamos el título. Ustedes conocen esta palabra. Léanla rápidamente la primera vez. Recuerden poner el dedo en la palabra mientras leen. Pongan el dedo en la palabra del título. *(Monitor.)*

Lean el título. *(Pause and tap.)* Isidro

Muy bien. Ahora lean el cuento. Listos. *(Pause. Start the timer, and tap.)*

Repeat the process with the entire story.

Note: Review any missed words.

(After reading the story the first time, ask students the following question:) **¿Acertaron en lo que sucedería en el cuento?** *(Discuss.)*

Individual Practice

(Call on individual students to read 1 or 2 pages. Do not tap during individual practice. Time students as a group. Note whether the group met the fluency goal on the Mastery Sheet.)

Part B: Retell

¿Qué pasa primero en este cuento? *(Call on students to retell the story in their words, 1 event at a time.)*

¡Muy bien! Marcaré esta actividad en la Hoja de maestría, y pasaremos a la actividad final de esta lección.

Lesson 78

Activity 6
What Do We Know?/
What Did We Learn?

(Use the ¿Qué sabemos?/¿Qué aprendimos? list created during the previous activity.)

Vamos a repasar la información que hemos escrito sobre los cocodrilos. Ahora que hemos leído el cuento *Isidro*, podemos determinar cuáles cosas son verdad y cuáles no son verdad.

(Draw a circle around the things that are true and cross out the things that are not true.)

Van a leer cada página del cuento y me dirán qué aprendieron de los cocodrilos en esa página.

Miren la primera página. ¿Qué aprendieron sobre los cocodrilos en esta página?

(Accept reasonable responses and write that information on the ¿Qué aprendimos? portion of the chart.)

Repeat the process with the entire story.

¡Aprendimos muchas cosas sobre los cocodrilos que no sabíamos antes!

¡Muy bien! Completaron esta actividad perfectamente. Marcaré esta actividad en la Hoja de maestría, y puedo poner un adhesivo en la Hoja de maestría de esta lección.

230 Lesson 78

Comprehension Strategies (Teacher's Edition B): Sentence Completion

Sentence completion tasks require students to complete sentences with the correct vocabulary word. Story vocabulary appears at the top of the page in a box in the **Activity Book.** By completing the sentences with the correct word, students demonstrate their understanding of key events in the story.

ACTIVITY AT A GLANCE

Scaffold instruction to assist students in selecting the correct vocabulary.

- Step 1: Students read the words that appear in the box.
- Step 2: Scaffold task difficulty by asking a question that will guide students in selecting the correct word. **¿Qué hace el mono? Sí, el mono canta. Escriban canta en el espacio. (What does the monkey do? Yes, the monkey sings. Write sing in the space provided.)**

- Step 3: If students do not select the correct vocabulary word, ask a question that will clarify which word is a better choice by reviewing the events in the related story. **¿Vuela el mono? No, el mono no vuela. No podemos escribir vuela en el espacio. ¿Quien vuela? Sí, el gato vuela. (Does the monkey fly? No, he doesn't. We can't write he flies in the sky. Who flies? Yes, the cat flies.)**
- Step 4: Have students read each sentence once it is completed to check for accuracy.

IN THE REAL WORLD

Although students may have experience with prior sentence completion activities, they may need assistance in deciding which word best completes the sentence. Ask guiding questions to help students remember what happened in the related story. Then complete the sentence with various words until the concept expressed in the sentence makes sense.

Questions and Answers

Lesson 56

Activity 7
Reading Comprehension

Part A: Sequencing

(You will use the marker board for this activity.)

**Vamos a hacer un resumen del cuento
¡Desear y poder! Aprendimos que si
tenemos el deseo de hacer una cosa,
tenemos el poder de hacerlo. Vamos a ver
cómo los diferentes animales en el cuento
tenían un deseo y pudieron lograrlo.**

*(Guide an oral discussion of the events that
occurred in the story. Write student responses on
the marker board.)*

**¿Qué pasa primero? El mono desea cantar.
¿Qué pasa después? La mosca desea pintar.
¿Qué pasa después? El yac desea leer.
¿Qué pasa después? El gato desea volar en
avión.**

**¿Qué pasa después? El pato desea tocar la
guitarra como un mariachi.**

*(Summarize the story from what you have written
on the marker board.)*

(Scaffold as necessary.)

¡Muy bien!

Part B: Sentence Completion

**Pasen a la página 37 en el *Libro de
actividades B*.**

**Ahora completen cada oración con la
palabra correcta.**

¿Qué hace el mono? canta
Sí, el mono canta. Entonces, escriban
canta **en el espacio.**
(Monitor and correct.)

(Scaffold as necessary.)

**Repeat the process until all the sentences
are complete.**

**Completaron esta actividad perfectamente.
Marcaré esta actividad en la Hoja de
maestría, y puedo poner un adhesivo en la
Hoja de maestría de esta lección.**

Lección 56

Actividad 7

toca	lee	canta
vuela		pinta

1. El mono **canta**.

2. La mosca **pinta**.

3. El yac **lee**.

4. El gato **vuela**.

5. El pato **toca** la guitarra.

Comprehension Strategies (Teacher's Edition C)

The activities covered in the Comprehension Strategies Strand in **Teacher's Edition C** come from six categories of comprehension strategies: Content Web, Vocabulary Building, What Do We Know?/What Did We Learn?, Sentence Completion, Main Idea, and Making Inferences. Unlike English phonology, there are fewer letters and corresponding sounds for students to learn in the Spanish language. In *SRA Intervenciones tempranas de la lectura,* students are ready early on to focus on using strategies to assist them in comprehending the stories they will read.

Comprehension Strategies (Teacher's Edition C): Content Web

Students learn to recall what they have learned from reading a story. A content web is used to organize the new information. Content webs that appear in the **Teacher's Editions** are for your reference only. The way they play out in the actual activity may very well be different.

ACTIVITY AT A GLANCE

- Step 1: Draw a circle in the center of the marker board. Write the story topic in the circle.
- Step 2: Ask probing questions about the story topic that students can answer from the story they just read.

- Step 3: Accept reasonable responses, and write the information on the marker board in circles branching off from the main circle.
- Step 4: Mastery is achieved when each student provides information from the story about the topic.

IN THE REAL WORLD

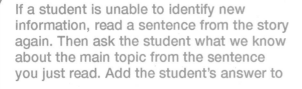

If a student is unable to identify new information, read a sentence from the story again. Then ask the student what we know about the main topic from the sentence you just read. Add the student's answer to the content web. Remember, content web responses in the **Teacher's Editions** are for reference only. Do not feel that the web you create for the activity must contain the same responses and information.

Questions and Answers

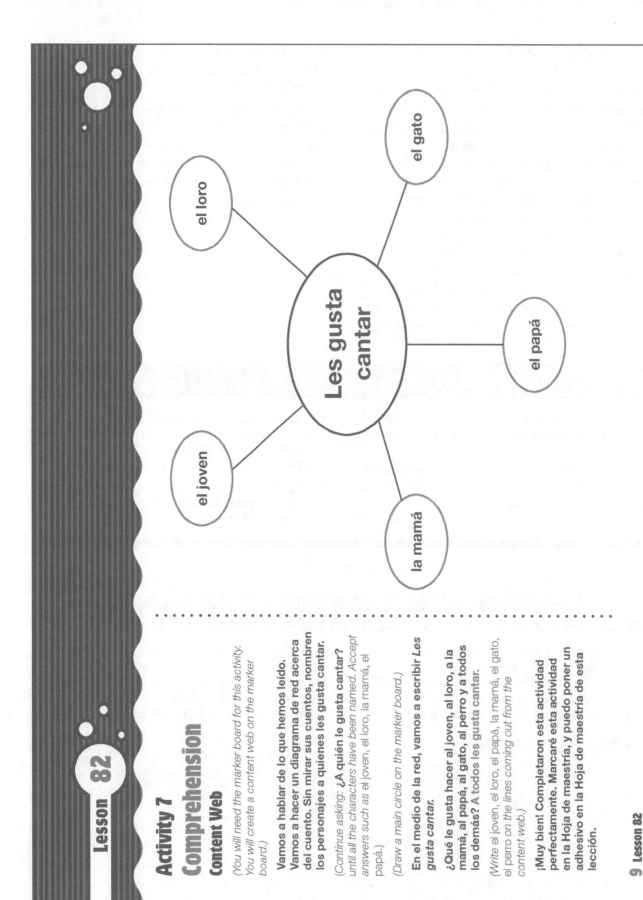

Activity 7
Comprehension
Content Web

(You will need the marker board for this activity. You will create a content web on the marker board.)

Vamos a hablar de lo que hemos leído. Vamos a hacer un diagrama de red acerca del cuento. Sin mirar sus cuentos, nombren los personajes a quienes les gusta cantar.

(Continue asking: ¿A quién le gusta cantar? until all the characters have been named. Accept answers such as el joven, el loro, la mamá, el papá.)

(Draw a main circle on the marker board.)

En el medio de la red, vamos a escribir Les gusta cantar.

¿Qué le gusta hacer al joven, al loro, a la mamá, al papá, al gato, al perro y a todos los demás? A todos les gusta cantar.

(Write el joven, el loro, el papá, la mamá, el gato, el perro on the lines coming out from the content web.)

¡Muy bien! Completaron esta actividad perfectamente. Marcaré esta actividad en la Hoja de maestría, y puedo poner un adhesivo en la Hoja de maestría de esta lección.

Comprehension Strategies (Teacher's Edition C): Vocabulary Building

The vocabulary building activity extends knowledge by introducing the meanings of words that are important for comprehending the story. Introducing and discussing the target words and meanings prior to reading the story prepares students to focus on understanding key concepts important for story comprehension. In later activities, students will be asked to write the new vocabulary words in their word journals.

ACTIVITY AT A GLANCE

- Step 1: Write the vocabulary words on the marker board.
- Step 2: Read the first word: **Van a aprender palabras nuevas. La primera palabra es pequeño. (You are going to learn new words. The first word is small.)**
- Step 3: Provide examples of the word as it is used in real life: **Los bebés son pequeños. Lo contrario a grande es pequeño. (Babies are small. Small is the opposite of big.)**
- Step 4: Repeat this process for each new vocabulary word.
- Step 5: Individual mastery is achieved when each student can identify the meaning of the words.

IN THE REAL WORLD

Because students enter school with varied levels of vocabulary knowledge, you should not assume that they will naturally understand the meanings of words and embedded concepts that appear in the stories. If children indicate that they are knowledgeable about specific words, they should be validated and given opportunities to use the word(s) in a meaningful way. Some children, however, may require several examples of the word used in context in order to learn the meaning of the word. If students have difficulty understanding a word meaning, a word that is opposite in meaning can also be introduced as a contrast. For example, when introducing the word **pequeño** (small), you can point to a large object in the classroom and then to a smaller object. The use of visuals, gestures, and real-life objects can help children understand the meanings of difficult words. Also, finding examples in the **Decodable Books** that illustrate the word meaning is a useful strategy to build word knowledge. Encourage students to use the vocabulary words to describe and make connections to real-life experiences in addition to discussing what they learned from the story. As students learn to record words in their word journals, encourage students to use the words throughout the day and to point out these words to you in any text they read in class.

Questions and Answers

Lesson 99

Activity 5
Decodable Book

Part A: Vocabulary

(Write pequeño on the marker board.)

Van a aprender una palabra nueva. La palabra es pequeño. *(Slide a finger under pequeño.)* **¿Cuál es la palabra?** pequeño

(Scaffold as necessary.)

Sí, la palabra es pequeño. Los bebés son pequeños. Lo contrario a grande es pequeño.

Individual Practice

(Provide individual practice.)

Part B: Fluency Development

(You will use a timer and marker board for this activity.)

*(Pass out **Libro decodificable 55,** El león pequeño, to students. Have students browse the text and make predictions. Solicit background information about lions—i.e. what the students know.)*

FLUENCY GOAL 91 words @ 49 wpm = 2 minutes

(Write ¿Qué sabemos? and ¿Qué aprendimos? on the marker board.)

¿Qué sabemos sobre los leones?
(Accept reasonable responses.)

¿Cómo viven los leones?
(Accept reasonable responses.)

¿Qué quiere hacer el leoncito?
(Accept reasonable responses.)

¿Qué hacen el papá y la mamá?
(Accept reasonable responses.)

(Write students' information under ¿Qué sabemos? on the marker board.)

Vamos a leer un texto informativo sobre un león.

Note: Provide no more than 1.5 seconds maximum think time per word.

Ahora leamos el título. Ustedes conocen estas palabras. Léanlas rápidamente la primera vez. Recuerden poner el dedo en cada palabra mientras leen. Pongan el dedo en la primera palabra del título. *(Monitor.)*

Lean el título. *(Pause and tap.)* **El** *(tap)* **león** *(tap)* **pequeño**

Muy bien. Ahora lean el texto informativo. Listos.
(Pause. Start the timer, and tap.)

Repeat the process with the entire story.

Note: Review any missed words.

(After reading the story the first time, ask students the following question:) **¿Acertaron en lo que sucedería en el texto informativo?** *(Discuss.)*

arrastra

comienza

delanteras

Lesson 101

(Write on the marker board any letter-sounds or words students had trouble with on Assessment 20. Using the model-lead-test strategy, review the letter-sounds and words with students.)

Activity 1
Vocabulary
Part A: Word Knowledge

(Hold up the book, and touch under the word arrastra.)

Ahora vamos a hablar sobre el significado de algunas de las palabras en nuestro cuento.
Lean la palabra. arrastra
Excelente. *Arrastra* es cuando llevas a una persona o cosa por el suelo o tiras de algo.

(As an example, give each student a pencil to drag across the table.)

(Then say:) **También puedo decir: *El gatito arrastra sus juguetes por el suelo.***

Lean la palabra. *(Touch under the next word.)* **comienza**

Excelente. *Comienza* significa que empieza algo o el principio de algo.

(As an example say:) ***La mamá gata empieza a darle alimento a sus gatitos.***

(Then say:) ***La mamá gata comienza a darle alimento a sus gatitos.***

Lean la palabra. *(Touch under the next word.)* **delanteras**
Excelente. *Delanteras* significa enfrente o adelante.

(As an example say:) **Si digo: *El gatito tiene sus patas de adelante sobre su cabeza.***

(Then say:) **También puedo decir: *El gatito tiene sus patas delanteras sobre su cabeza.***

Part B: Word Journal

(Have students write the new vocabulary words in their word journals. Remind students that they should point out these words to you in any text they read in class. Have students place the word journal page in their folders.)

Ya sabemos los significados de las palabras *arrastra*, *comienza* y *delanteras*. Cuando leamos el cuento, quiero que presten atención a estas tres palabras. Cuando las vean u oigan, levanten la mano.

¡Muy bien! Aprendieron el significado de las palabras nuevas. Marcaré esta actividad en la Hoja de maestría, y podemos pasar a la siguiente actividad.

106 **Lesson 101**

Comprehension Strategies (Teacher's Edition C): What Do We Know?/What Did We Learn? (¿Qué sabemos?/ ¿Qué aprendimos?)

This comprehension strategy appeared in **Teacher's Edition B.** The What Do We Know? part of the activity now sometimes appears as the first task in the Fluency Development activities. Make a chart to record student responses before and after reading the story: **¿Qué sabemos?/ ¿Qué aprendimos? (What do we know?/What did we learn?).** Follow the same procedure as in **Teacher's Edition B:** Discuss and record what students already know about a topic prior to reading. Then, identify new information they learned after reading the story.

ACTIVITY AT A GLANCE

- Step 1: Write the topic at the top of the marker board.
- Step 2: Draw two columns on the marker board. On the left side write **¿Qué sabemos? (What do we know?).** On the right side write **¿Qué aprendimos? (What did we learn?)**
- Step 3: Ask students what they already know about the topic.
- Step 4: Write the students answers in the left column under **¿Qué sabemos? (What do we know?)** (Do not erase the information in this column. You will use this chart in the next lesson.)

- Step 5: Read the story.
- Step 6: Review the information written in the left column under **¿Qué sabemos? (What do we know?)**
- Step 7: Draw a circle around things that are true. Cross out the things that are not.
- Step 8: Read each page of the story. Students report what they learned.
- Step 9: Summarize the information.
- Step 10: Individual mastery for comprehension is achieved by letting each student take a turn telling what he or she learned from a page in the story.

IN THE REAL WORLD

One important scaffold in this activity is reviewing what students already know and drawing a circle around the statements that are true and crossing out the statements that are not true. In this way, misconceptions about a topic are addressed early on and students' factual knowledge of the world is extended. This activity can generalize into similar tasks across the day when children are asked to identify true and false statements during content learning (e.g., science and social studies). When students cannot agree about whether a statement is true or not, encourage them to provide a reason for their thinking. This should generate a discussion in which you can provide further information on the topic so that students can then develop a deeper understanding about the topic. This may require that you briefly read about the topic prior to teaching the lesson.

Questions and Answers

Lesson 99

Activity 5
Decodable Book

Part A: Vocabulary

(Write pequeño *on the marker board.)*

Van a aprender una palabra nueva. La palabra es *pequeño*. *(Slide a finger under* pequeño*.)* **¿Cuál es la palabra?**
pequeño

(Scaffold as necessary.)

Sí, la palabra es *pequeño*. Lo contrario a *grande* es *pequeño*. Los bebés son pequeños. Lo contrario a *grande* es *pequeño*.

Individual Practice

(Provide individual practice.)

Part B: Fluency Development

(You will use a timer and marker board for this activity.)

*(Pass out **Libro decodificable 55**,* El león pequeño, *to students. Have students browse the text and make predictions. Solicit background information about lions — i.e. what the students know.)*

FLUENCY GOAL 91 words @ 49 wpm = 2 minutes

(Write ¿Qué sabemos? *and* ¿Qué aprendimos? *on the marker board.)*

¿Qué sabemos sobre los leones?
(Accept reasonable responses.)

¿Cómo viven los leones?
(Accept reasonable responses.)

¿Qué quiere hacer el leoncito?
(Accept reasonable responses.)

¿Qué hacen el papá y la mamá?
(Accept reasonable responses.)

(Write students' information under ¿Qué sabemos? *on the marker board.)*

Vamos a leer un texto informativo sobre un león.

Note: Provide no more than 1.5 seconds maximum think time per word.

Ahora leamos el título. Ustedes conocen estas palabras. Léanlas rápidamente la primera vez. Recuerden poner el dedo en cada palabra mientras leen. Pongan el dedo en la primera palabra del título.
(Monitor.)

Lean el título. *(Pause and tap.)* **El** *(tap)* **león** *(tap)* pequeño

Muy bien. Ahora lean el texto informativo. Listos.
(Pause. Start the timer, and tap.)

Repeat the process with the entire story.

Note: Review any missed words.

(After reading the story the first time, ask students the following question:) **¿Acertaron en lo que sucedería en el texto informativo?**
(Discuss.)

Lesson 100

Activity 2

What Do We Know?/
What Did We Learn?

(Use the ¿Qué sabemos?/¿Qué aprendimos? information written on the marker board from the previous lesson.)

Vamos a repasar la información que hemos escrito en la lección anterior sobre los leones. Ahora que hemos leído el texto informativo *El león pequeño*, podemos determinar cuáles cosas son verdad y cuáles no son verdad.

(Draw a circle around the things that are true and cross out the things that are not true.)

Van a leer cada página del texto informativo y me dirán qué aprendieron sobre los leones en cada página.

Miren la primera página. ¿Qué aprendieron sobre los leones en esta página?

(Accept reasonable responses and write that information on the ¿Qué aprendimos? portion of the chart.)

Repeat the process with the entire text.

Aprendimos muchas cosas sobre los leones que no sabíamos antes.

¡Muy bien! Puedo marcar esta actividad en la Hoja de maestría, y podemos pasar a la siguiente actividad.

101 Lesson 100

Comprehension Strategies (Teacher's Edition C): Reading Comprehension: Sentence Completion

Students were introduced to Sentence Completion activities in **Teacher's Edition B.** Sentence completion tasks require students to complete sentences with the correct vocabulary word. Story vocabulary appears at the top of the page in a box in the **Libro de actividades.** By completing the sentences with the correct word, students demonstrate their understanding of key events in the story.

ACTIVITY AT A GLANCE

Scaffold instruction to assist students in selecting the correct vocabulary.

- Step 1: Students read the words that appear in the box.
- Step 2: Students read the sentences.
- Step 3: Students write the correct word in the blank.

- Step 4: Students read each of the completed sentences out loud.
- Step 5: If students did not select the correct vocabulary word, scaffold by asking a question that will clarify which word is a better choice. Check for accuracy.

Lesson 88

Activity 2
Reading Comprehension

Pasen a la página 11 en el *Libro de actividades C.*

Observen sus cuadernos. Hay seis oraciones con un espacio en blanco. Tienen que completarlas con una de las palabras del recuadro. *(Point to the words in the box and the blanks in the sentences.)*

Primero lean rápidamente las palabras del recuadro. *(Monitor to see that students are pointing to the words at the top of the page.)*

Listos. *(Pause.)*

Pongan el dedo en la primera palabra. Piensen en los sonidos. *(Allow students 2 seconds of think time.)*

Lean la palabra. mira

(Scaffold as necessary.)

> **Repeat the process with the following words: pregunta, marcha, alcalde, está, atranca.**

Ahora van a leer la primera oración. *(Tap softly for each word.)*

Escriban la palabra apropiada en el espacio.

(Monitor and correct.)

> **Repeat the process with the remaining sentences.**

(Scaffold as necessary.)

Lean las oraciones con las respuestas correctas. Listos.

Lean la primera oración. Un pavo real está en la plaza.

> **Repeat the process with the remaining sentences.**

(Scaffold as necessary.)

¡Buen trabajo! Ahora puedo marcar esta actividad en la Hoja de maestría, y podemos pasar a la siguiente actividad. Dejen el libro de actividades abierto porque lo usaremos más tarde.

Lección 88

Actividad 2

mira	pregunta	marcha
alcalde	está	atranca

1. Un pavo real **está** en la plaza.

2. La gente **mira** el pavo real.

3. El pavo real **atranca** el tráfico.

4. El alcalde **pregunta**: ¿De quién es este pavo?

5. El **alcade** da una hora para sacar el pavo de la plaza.

6. El pavo real **marcha** con Pablo.

Libro de actividades C

11

Comprehension Strategies (Teacher's Edition C): Main Idea/Sentence Dictation

The ability to identify the main idea allows the reader to identify the main theme of a story. Students often include unnecessary information when stating the main theme of a story. Often it can sound more like a brief summary of the story. The basic strategy to use is to ask students to first name whom or what the story is mainly about. Then ask students to talk about the most important thing they learned about who or what. The main idea of a story usually includes the main character, the problem, and its outcome.

ACTIVITY AT A GLANCE

- Step 1: Students identify *whom* or *what* is the story about. **¿Sobre quién trata el cuento? (Who is the story about?)**

- Step 2: Students identify what is the most important thing that was learned about the *who* or *what.* **¿Qué sucede en el cuento? (What happened in the story?)** For example, **¿Qué pueden hacer los gatitos? Sí, los gatitos juegan independientemente de su mamá. (How do the kittens play? Yes, they play independently from their mother.)**

- Step 3: Identify the main idea of the story. Say, **¿Cuál es la idea principal del cuento? Sí, la idea principal es *Los gatitos pueden jugar independientemente de su mamá.* (What is the main idea of the story? Yes, the main idea is that the kittens can play independently from their mother.)**

- Step 4: Students restate the main idea in as few words as possible.

- Step 5: Model stating the main idea in very few words.

- Step 6: Teacher and students repeat the main idea sentence together.

- Step 7: Students write the main idea in the **Libro de actividades.** Monitor and scaffold to ensure students write the words in the correct order You may need to use the marker board as a scaffold.

- Step 8: Individual mastery is achieved if each student can demonstrate understanding of the main idea and can state it using only a few words.

IN THE REAL WORLD

This is a very challenging task for students. They may need a lot of scaffolding. If students have difficulty in identifying the main idea, use the following process. Use a story the students have read that appeared in **Teacher's Edition B.** Ask whom or what the story is about. Ask what happened to the who or what in the story.

After students identify the main idea in the story, they might include unnecessary details when they state the main idea. You will need to help students see which information needs to be left in and which information can be taken out. For example, using the same story that students read and that was discussed in **Teacher's Edition B,** help students see which information is unnecessary for stating the main idea. Students can continue to work on stating the main idea in ten words or fewer in future stories. In the beginning, you need to let them know that you are looking for the most important information and nothing extra.

Questions and Answers

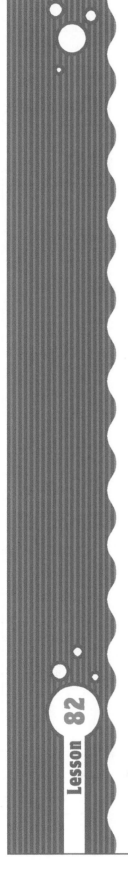

Activity 2
Main Idea
Sentence Dictation

Ahora que leyeron *La araña*, díganme: ¿cuál es la idea principal del cuento? La telaraña de Fili es toda su vida.

(Scaffold as necessary.)

¿Qué le pasó a la araña? El balón dañó su tela. Sí, eso pasó. ¿Qué más? La araña teje otra tela en lo alto de un árbol.

Muy bien.

Miren los espacios para la actividad 2 en la página 2 del *Libro de actividades C*.

Vamos a escribir la idea principal en una oración.

Escuchen. La idea principal es *La telaraña de Fili es toda su vida.*

Esta oración es la idea principal del cuento. Repítanla conmigo.

(Teacher and students:) La telaraña de Fili es toda su vida.

Ahora van a escribirla. ¿Qué ponemos al final de una oración? un punto

Muy bien.

(Praise those who remembered. Scaffold those who forgot.)

Repitan la oración solos. La telaraña de Fili es toda su vida.

Ahora escríbanla en sus cuadernos en el orden en que la dijeron.

¡Excelente! Hemos terminado otra actividad, y puedo marcar la caja para esta actividad en la Hoja de maestría.

Dejen el libro de actividades abierto porque lo usaremos más tarde.

Lección 82

Actividad 2

La telaraña de Fili es toda su vida.

Actividad 4

baño	noche	canta
ocho	casa	año
techo	coche	plaza

Libro de actividades C

Lesson 104

Activity 2
Main Idea
Sentence Dictation

Miren los espacios para la actividad 2 en el *Libro de actividades C.*

Hoy vamos a hablar sobre la idea principal del cuento y después van a escribir una oración. La idea principal consiste en dos partes: la primera es sobre qué o sobre quién trata el cuento. La segunda es lo que sucede o pasa en el cuento.

¿Sobre quién trata el cuento? los gatitos
¿Qué pueden hacer los gatitos? jugar sin su mamá

(Scaffold as necessary.)

Buen trabajo.

Vamos a escribir la idea principal en una oración.

Escuchen. La idea principal es *Los gatitos pueden jugar sin su mamá.*
Esta oración es la idea principal del cuento.
Repítanla conmigo.

(Teacher and students:) **Los gatitos pueden jugar sin su mamá.**

Ahora van a escribirla. ¿Qué ponemos al final de una oración? un punto

Muy bien.

(Praise those who remembered, scaffold those who forgot.)

Repitan la oración ustedes solos. Los gatitos pueden jugar sin su mamá.
Ahora escríbanla en sus cuadernos en el orden en que la dijeron.

¡Muy buen trabajo!

Marcaré esta actividad en la Hoja de maestría, y podemos pasar a la siguiente actividad.

123 Lesson 104

Lección 104

Actividad 1

banquillo   regañarlos

principio   después

alimento   cazaran

Actividad 2

Los gatitos pueden jugar sin su mamá.

Comprehension Strategies (Teacher's Edition C): Making Inferences

Making inferences helps students better understand what they are reading. When making inferences, students use prior knowledge and textual clues to draw conclusions beyond what is stated directly in the text.

In this activity students review three facts from a selection they have read. The teacher then explores the relationships between these facts in order to demonstrate how to infer new information.

ACTIVITY AT A GLANCE

- Step 1: Tell students that what they learn when they read can be used as clues to help them figure out other things.

- Step 2: Review the facts from the story read in the previous lesson. The teacher can reread the text to identify the facts that students will draw an inference from.

- Step 3: The teacher identifies the three facts. Students write these facts in their **Libro de actividades.** Monitor and scaffold as students write the sentences on the lines.

- Step 4: The teacher states a rule, putting the facts together, that can be used for making other inferences. For example, **Todos los mamíferos tienen estas tres características. Vamos a usar las características para decidir si estos animales son mamíferos también. (All mammals have these three characteristics. We will use the characteristics to decide if these animals are also mammals.)**

- Step 5; Model how to use the three facts to make other inferences. For example, **Los perros son mamíferos. Lo sabemos porque tienen las tres características de un mamífero. (Dogs are mammals. We know because they have the three characteristics of a mammal.)**

- Step 6: Individual mastery is achieved by each student demonstrating that they understand the process for making inferences to create new facts.

IN THE REAL WORLD

Listen closely to students' responses. Their responses will let you know what they are thinking. Do students understand what a mammal is? In order to make inferences accurately, students need to clearly understand the three facts they are putting together to make the new fact.

Check student understanding for making inferences by stating the new fact and then asking students how they know it to be true, because it is not directly stated in the text. Students should be able to identify clues in the text that support the new fact.

Questions and Answers

Lesson 101

Activity 4
Comprehension
Making Inferences

(You will use Tarjetas de sonido: 12, 17, 19, 25: ll—iguana, Ll ll—llama, rr—perro, Ch ch—chicharra.)

(Have students turn to page 2 of the reading selection Cómo crecen los gatitos *in the* Edición del Estudiante *and look at the picture.)*

Miren los espacios para la actividad 4 en el *Libro de actividades C.*

En la última actividad, leímos sobre el nacimiento de los gatitos. Ahora vamos a inferir nueva información basándonos en el cuento. El cuento nos dice que cada uno de los gatitos gatea hacia el cuerpo calentito de la mamá. El cuento también nos dice que los gatitos toman leche del cuerpo de su mamá. Como estas dos son características de un mamífero, sabemos que los gatos son mamíferos.

Estas son tres características de un mamífero.
1. Un mamífero tiene la sangre caliente.
2. Los bebés de mamíferos nacen vivos.
3. La mamá alimenta a su bebé con leche de su cuerpo.

(Scaffold as necessary).

Muy bien. Todos los mamíferos tienen estas tres características.

Ahora vamos a usar las características para decidir si estos animales son mamíferos.

(Hold up the rr *Tarjeta de sonido, and point to the picture of the dog.)*

Cuando tocas un perro, ¿se siente caliente? Sí.
Hagan una palomita en el cuadro. Entonces, ¿un perro tiene sangre caliente? Sí.
Hagan una palomita en el cuadro.
Cuando los cachorros nacen, ¿nacen vivos? Sí.
¿Es verdad que la mamá de los cachorros los alimenta con leche de su cuerpo? Sí.
Hagan una palomita en el cuadro.

¿Son los perros mamíferos? Sí.

Escriban *sí* en el cuadro debajo de *perros.*

Los perros son mamíferos. Lo sabemos porque tienen las tres características.

> **Repeat the process with the remaining animals.**

¡Perfecto, determinaron cuáles animales son mamíferos! Ahora puedo marcar esta actividad en la Hoja de maestría, y podemos pasar a la siguiente actividad.

Lección 101

Actividad 2

comienza lamerlos pequeñito

calorcillo delanteras despacito

arrastra encuentran

Actividad 4

	perro	llama	chicharra	iguana
1. ¿Tiene la sangre caliente?	✔	✔		
2. ¿Nacen vivos los bebés?	✔	✔		
3. ¿Es verdad que la mamá lo alimenta con leche de su cuerpo?	✔	✔		
¿Es un mamífero, sí o no?	sí	sí	no	no

Libro de actividades C

31

Guidelines for Teaching the First Lesson in SRA Intervenciones tempranas de la lectura

Activity 1: Rules

SRA Intervenciones tempranas de la lectura **Rules:** It is important to begin by explaining the three rules: **Siéntense derechos. (Sit tall.) Eschuchen atentamente. (Listen closely.) Contesten juntos cuando les dé la señal. (Answer when I give the signal.)** State the rule, and model the correct behavior. You may add additional rules at your own discretion. For example: **Los ojos aquí. (Eyes on me.)**

Cues: Tell the students that a cue is something you will do to tell them when to answer. Explain to the students what types of cues you plan to use. Sometimes the activity will include instructions regarding what cue to use, other times it will not. When the cue is not specified, you may select an appropriate cue. You may want to nod your head after asking a question students are supposed to answer, you may want to drop your hand after asking the question, or you may want to use a spoken cue after asking a question. The choice is yours, but consistency is essential to ensure students learn to watch for your cue and understand when to respond.

Merits of Becoming a Better Reader: Discuss with your students the merits of becoming a better reader. There are many reasons for wanting to become a better reader. Reading is fun; reading helps you to do your homework; reading helps you understand directions; reading helps you learn about anything you are interested in, such as bikes, skateboards, sports, or music; and reading helps you know how to follow a recipe, how to put a model together, and learn other skills. Ask the students for their ideas and reasons for the importance of learning how to read well.

Mastery Sheet: Hold up the first Mastery Sheet, and show it to the students. Down the left column are the Lesson numbers. One lesson is conducted each day. Within the lesson there are several activities. Some lessons have six or seven activities; others might have eight, nine, or ten. You will place a check mark in the appropriate box after each activity is mastered. Once all the boxes are checked for the lesson, place a sticker (You might call it **un adhesivo/una etiqueta.**) in the last box to indicate that the students have mastered that lesson. You should show excitement about rewarding the sticker at the end of a mastered lesson, because this indicates the students' success. If the lesson is not completed during the assigned time frame, start with the unfinished activity or activities before starting the next lesson.

Praise: Make positive feedback specific to students' behavior. For example, **Buen trabajo diciendo los sonidos,** instead of just saying **Buen trabajo.**

Activity 2: First-Sound Game

In this activity, you will say a word, emphasizing the first sound in the word. This means you should hold the first sound for two or three seconds before saying the rest of the word. **/Mmm/esa.** This helps the students hear the first sound. (The same procedure applies to later activities stressing the ending sound.) It is crucial that the sounds are held for an extended time if the students are going to benefit from this activity. Emphasizing the first sound allows the students to hear the separate phoneme within the word.

Activity 3:
Letter-Sound Introduction

Use the *Mm* letter-sound card to introduce the sound of the letter *m*. Remember to hold the sound for at least two or three seconds. When you read the Mango poem, stretch all the /mmm/ sounds. During the second reading, have the students say the /mmm/ part with you.

Activity 4: Thumbs Up-Thumbs Down Game: First Sound

This is an auditory activity in which the students listen to the first sound in a given word and determine if the word begins with a specified letter-sound (in this lesson the sound is /mmm/). As in Activity 2, you are instructed to emphasize the first sound in the word. This means you should hold the first sound for two or three seconds before saying the rest of the word. You should have the students practice putting their thumbs up, putting their thumbs down, and placing their hands flat on the table as they would between words.

Activity 5: Writing the Letter.

Review formation of the letter before modeling how to write it. The students' letters should be legible; however, the activity should not be turned into a penmanship lesson. If your school has its own writing system, use that system when modeling letter formation.

When the dialogue directs you to demonstrate how to write a letter, model writing the letter on the marker board, on the board, or on a copy of the activity sheet.

Activity 6: Stretch the Word Game

When stretching words, it is very important that you do *not* stop between sounds. Each individual sound should blend into the next. It is equally important that you do *not* hold stop sounds, as this would distort the sound. Finally, it is imperative that you do *not* add any sounds to the end of stop sounds, as this would again be a distortion of the true sound. For example, the sound of the letter b is /b/ and not /buh/. When stretching words and using your visual cues, it is important that you do **NOT** mouth the sounds. Since this is the first time the students are being asked to perform this skill, it is important that they learn the procedures correctly. Take the time to train them on the correct visual cues, since they will be asked to perform this skill throughout the curriculum.

Activity 7: Phonological Awareness/Listening to Syllables

In this auditory activity, students will learn that words can be divided into syllables. Model the procedure by saying the word. Pause and give students time to think about what they heard, and then say the syllables in the word, clapping for each syllable. Say the word again and have students practice saying **ma** *(clap)* **ma** *(clap)*. Providing an instructional cue here is important because it will allow the students to respond in unison as you monitor to observe if each student is able to hear and say each syllable. Then have students say the word as a group and say each syllable within the word with a clap. This activity is similar to stretching a word into individual phonemes. This activity allows the student to hear each separate syllable in a word.

Activity 8:
Phonological Awareness/Building Syllables

The point of this auditory activity is to teach students how to form syllables. Students learn that a syllable is a part of a word. Syllables are formed when a consonant and vowel sound are united. Although we do not use the terms *consonant* and *vowel,* students will learn to build a syllable with two sounds or phonemes, for example: **/mmm/** and **/aaa/.** It is important to use the Mm sound card to review the sound for the letter. Touch under the letter and have students give the sound, holding it for two or three seconds. Now model saying the sound **/mmm/** and the second sound **/aaa/.** Hold each sound for two or three seconds each so that students can hear each phoneme. Say the syllable **ma,** explaining that when you join **/mmm/** with **/aaa/** you form the syllable **ma.** Have the students now practice with you, producing and holding each sound individually and then joining them to form the syllable **ma.** Then have students perform the task as a group, giving them a cue for responding in unison. The Model-Lead-Test procedure used in this activity allows you to monitor students' ability to hear individual phonemes that form a syllable.

Activity 9:
Oral Blending/Say the Word Game

In this activity, you will use Pepe the puppet to demonstrate how to blend individual phonemes to form a word. Students learn that Pepe has difficulty saying words correctly. He likes to stretch words slowly. The goal of this game is for students to listen to Pepe, who stretches each individual sound in a word, and to blend the sounds together and say the word. This auditory task can be challenging for students who must hear each sound in the word before blending them together and saying the word. It is important that you encourage the students to listen carefully to Pepe to understand what word he stretched. Demonstrate the process by whispering a word to Pepe: **ama.** Tell the students to listen carefully. Move the puppet's lips and stretch the sounds in the word: **/aaa/mmm/aaa/.** Hold each sound for two or three seconds. When stretching words, it is very important that you do not stop between sounds. Ask students what word did Pepe stretch—**ama.** Now have students listen again as Pepe stretches the sounds in the same word. Provide a cue to signal for students to "say the word" with you. It is important that in the individual practice, each student has an opportunity to say a word that Pepe has stretched.

Concluding the Lesson

Be sure to check the Mastery Sheet after each activity has been completed. When the entire lesson has been mastered, let the students know how proud you are of them for doing such a great job. Be specific in your praise, for example, **¡Buen trabajo diciendo el primer sonido que escuchan en las palabras! (Good job saying the first sound that you hear in the words!)** Place a sticker on the Mastery Sheet, collect materials, and move to the next lesson or dismiss students, as appropriate.

Sample Lessons

Here are three sample lessons, one from each **Teacher's Edition.** These lessons show how the skills integrate and develop throughout the curriculum.

Lesson 1

MATERIALS

1. Tarjeta de sonido 1 (Mm)
2. *Libro de actividades A*, page 1
3. Marker Board
4. Pepe

OBJECTIVES

Activity 1 *Rules*
• Establish rules

Activity 2 *Phonemic Awareness*
• Identify the position of a sound in a word

Activity 3 *Letter-Sound Correspondences*
• Learn the sound of the letter *m*
• Associate sounds with letters
• Listen for and identify the /m/ sound in a poem

Activity 4 *Phonemic Awareness*
• Identify the position of a sound in a word

Activity 5 *Letter-Sound Correspondences*
• Learn the correct strokes for writing lowercase letters
• Match the sounds of letters to printed letters

Activity 6 *Phonemic Awareness*
• Segment spoken words into sounds
• Understand that each finger represents one sound in a word

Activity 7 *Word Recognition and Spelling*
• Segment words into syllables

Activity 8 *Phonemic Awareness*
• Blend phonemes to form syllables

Activity 9 *Phonemic Awareness*
• Blend phonemes to say words

Activity 1
Rules

Buenos días. Mi nombre es _____. Soy el/la maestro(a) de lectura. Este año voy a enseñarles a leer bien. Saber leer es importante para toda la vida. Antes de empezar la primera lección, vamos a aprendernos los nombres de todos para conocernos mejor. *(Take a few moments to find out students' names, and let them say hello to each other.)*

(Start with any student.) **¿Cuál es tu nombre?** *(Student answer. To the whole class:)* **Díganle "hola [student name]" a [student name].** *(Repeat with all the other students).*

Ya que sabemos nuestros nombres, necesitamos platicar sobre algunas cosas más.

Vamos a trabajar juntos en lectura todos los días.

Existen unas reglas de comportamiento que debemos seguir para trabajar en grupo y son las siguientes:

(Explain and model each of the following rules:)

Siéntense derechos. *(Have students demonstrate this rule.)* **Muéstrenme que pueden sentarse derechos.** *(Students should sit up straight.)*

Escuchen atentamente.

Contesten juntos cuando les dé la señal. *(Show students a cue, such as hand up like a stop sign. Explain the cue as you demonstrate.)* **Esto significa que tienen que detenerse y escuchar.**

(Put your hand down and demonstrate the cue again while saying:) **Deténganse. Escuchen.** *(Have students demonstrate the cue with you.)* **Háganlo conmigo.** *(Monitor and correct if necessary.)*

(Demonstrate the hand-drop cue. Hold your hand at shoulder level with your palm facing outward. Give approximately two seconds of think time, and then drop your hand with a slashing motion indicating that you are ready for the students' answer.) **Esto significa que tienen que contestar una pregunta.**

(Have students demonstrate the cue with you.) **Háganlo conmigo.** *(Monitor, and correct if necessary.)*

(Demonstrate a verbal request for a response.) **Cuando diga listo, tienen que prepararse para responder. Vamos a intentarlo.** *(Ask a student:)* **Listo. ¿Cuál es tu nombre?** *(Student should respond with his or her name.)*

¡Muy bien!

Lesson 1

(You may want to show non-examples.)

Ahora vamos a practicar las reglas.
Vamos a practicar cómo contestar juntos cuando les dé la señal. *(Hold up the book so students can see the pictures. Touch under the monkey.)*

Voy a hacerles unas preguntas sobre estos dibujos. ¿Es un mono? *(Pause. Cue students, using the hand-drop cue.)* **Sí.**
(Repeat if students did not answer together.)

Siguiente.

(Touch under the dog.) **¿Es un gato?** *(Pause. Cue students using the hand-drop cue.)* **No.**
(Touch under the girl.) **¿Es un gato?** *(Pause. Cue students using the hand-drop cue.)* **No.**
(Touch under the cat.) **¿Es un gato?** *(Pause. Cue students using the hand-drop cue.)* **Sí.**
(Repeat until all students answer on cue.)

¡Buen trabajo contestando al darles la señal!

(Praise students, and continue.)

Cuando trabajen juntos y sigan las reglas, leerán mejor.

(Discuss the merits of becoming a better reader. You may want to ask:) **¿Por qué es importante leer bien?**

(Discuss the merits of becoming a better reader.)

Leer es divertido.
Saber leer bien les ayudará a aprender.
Saber leer bien les ayudará con las tareas.
Saber leer bien les ayudará cuando estén jugando algunos juegos.

(Explain the mastery measurement system throughout the rest of the lesson. Hold up the Mastery Sheet for this lesson and show it to students. Point to each item as you explain it.)

Esto es la Hoja de maestría.
Éstas son nuestras lecciones.
Cada día vamos hacer una lección.

Hay muchas actividades en cada lección. Estas actividades fueron hechas para ayudarles a aprender a leer. La cantidad de actividades cambia de un día a otro.

Hay una caja para cada actividad. Voy a poner una marca en la caja cuando hayan terminado la actividad correctamente. Cuando todas las cajas de una lección estén completas, pondré un adhesivo en la última caja. Esto quiere decir que han aprendido todas las habilidades de la lección.

Si no terminamos la lección en un día, terminaremos las actividades al día siguiente antes de continuar con la siguiente lección.

Ahora, ya que hemos terminado esta actividad, marco la caja de esta actividad y podemos pasar a la siguiente.

Lesson 1

Activity 2
First-Sound Game

Ahora vamos a hacer algo diferente. Voy a decir una palabra. Cuando lo indique, ustedes digan el primer sonido que escuchen en la palabra. Ésta es la señal que utilizaré. *(Demonstrate holding up one finger.)* Haré una primero.

Mi turno. La primera palabra es *mesa*. *(Pause.)* /Mmm/esa. *(Pause.)*
¿Cuál es el primer sonido que escucho en *mesa*? /Mmm/.
Háganlo conmigo. Escuchen. *Mesa.* *(Pause.)* /Mmm/esa. *(Pause.)*
¿Cuál es el primer sonido que escuchamos?
(Teacher and students:) /mmm/

Ahora, ustedes solos. Voy a decir una palabra. Cuando lo indique, ustedes digan el primer sonido que escuchen en la palabra. Recuerden contestar juntos cuando lo indique.
La primera palabra es *mesa. Mesa.* *(Pause.)* /Mmm/esa.

¿Cuál es el primer sonido que escuchan en *mesa*? *(Cue students by holding up one finger. This cue is related to the hand cue you will use in the stretching activities.)* /mmm/

Sí, el primer sonido en *mesa* es /mmm/.

Siguiente palabra. *Mamá.* *(Pause.)* /Mmm/amá. *(Pause.)*
¿Cuál es el primer sonido? *(Cue students by holding up one finger.)* /mmm/

Repeat the process with the following words: **ama, sol, me, mango, amigo, salsa.**

(Scaffold as necessary. Use the model-lead-test strategy when a student makes a mistake.)

ERROR CORRECTION:
Mi turno. *(Say the sound of the beginning letter of the word where the error occurred for 2 seconds.)* **El primer sonido en la palabra _____ es _____.**
(Ask all students to repeat the sound.)
Ahora, ustedes juntos. *(Possible student responses: /aaa/ , /sss/ , /mmm/.)*
Ahora vamos a hacerlo otra vez. *(Back up 2 items and restart the activity.)*

Individual Practice
(Provide individual practice with 2 or 3 words per student.)

¡Buen trabajo diciendo el primer sonido que escuchan en las palabras!
Han terminado esta actividad. Ahora puedo marcar la caja para esta actividad en la Hoja de maestría.

Activity 3

Letter-Sound Introduction

Cuando leemos, usamos las letras para formar palabras.

(Hold up Mm Tarjeta de sonido with the capital M covered. Touch under m.)

¿Cuál es el nombre de esta letra? *(Touch under m.)* m

(Provide the name of the letter to students if they don't know it.) **¡Muy bien! Esta letra es la m. Vamos a aprender el sonido de esta letra. Cada letra representa un sonido. Los sonidos de las letras nos ayudan a leer palabras. El sonido de esta letra es /mmm/.**

Díganlo conmigo. ¿Cuál es el sonido de esta letra? *(Touch under m.)* /mmm/ *(Teacher and students:)* /mmm/

Otra vez. Digan el sonido de esta letra conmigo. *(Touch under m.)* /mmm/ *(Teacher and students:)* /mmm/

Ahora ustedes. ¿Cuál es el sonido? *(Touch under m.)* /mmm/

(Praise students.)

¡Muy bien! El sonido de esta letra es /mmm/.

Individual Practice

(Provide individual practice.)

La tarjeta del mango nos ayudará a recordar el sonido de la letra m. Todos. ¿Cuál es el primer sonido en /mmm/ango? *(Cue students by using the point-touch cue.)* /mmm/

Cuando escribimos mango, /mmm/ es el sonido de la primera letra.

(Point to the word mango at bottom of the card. Ask each student:) **¿Cuál es el sonido de esta letra?** *(Touch under m.)* /mmm/

Cada vez que aprendamos una letra, usaremos una Tarjeta de sonido para ayudarnos a recordar su sonido. Después de aprender la letra y su sonido pondremos la Tarjeta de sonido en la pared.

Voy a leer un poema. Quiero que ustedes escuchen las palabras porque algunas comienzan con el sonido /mmm/.

(Read the following poem.)

**Miguel Montes fue al mercado el martes por la mañana.
"Mmm, mmm, mmm", dijo Miguel mientras miraba las frutas.**

**Él compró muchos mangos.
"Mmm, mmm, mmm",
dice Miguel mientras come los mangos en su mesa.**

**"¡Qué ricos son!", dice Miguel.
"Mmm, mmm, mmm".**

¿Qué decía Miguel cuando comía los mangos? *(Cue.)* /mmm/ /mmm/ /mmm/

Voy a leer el poema de nuevo. Escuchen las palabras que comienzan con /mmm/.

(Read the poem again, emphasizing the beginning sound of words that begin with the letter m.)

¿Cuáles palabras comienzan con el sonido /mmm/? *(Accept reasonable responses, such as Miguel, Montes, mercado, martes, mañana, mientras, miraba, muchos, mangos, mesa.)*

(Praise students, and place the Mm Tarjeta de sonido on the wall.)

¡Buen trabajo encontrando las palabras que comienzan con el sonido /mmm/! Ahora vamos a poner la Tarjeta de sonido en la pared para que nos recuerde su sonido.

Han terminado esta actividad. Ahora puedo marcar la caja para esta actividad en la Hoja de maestría. Gracias por escuchar tan bien, sentarse derechos y contestar todos juntos.

Lesson 1

Activity 4

Thumbs Up–Thumbs Down Game

Mm

En esta actividad vamos a jugar a "¿Pulgares arriba o abajo?".

Voy a decir una palabra y quiero que escuchen si comienza con el sonido /mmm/.

(Hold up the Mm Tarjeta de sonido. Touch under m.)

¿Cuál sonido van a escuchar? *(Touch under m.) /mmm/*

Correcto. Escuchen si comienza con el sonido /mmm/. Jugaremos a este juego de este modo. Voy a decir una palabra. Si la palabra comienza con el sonido /mmm/, apunten su pulgar hacia arriba.

(Demonstrate a thumbs-up.)

¿Qué van a hacer cuando escuchan el sonido /mmm/ al principio de la palabra? *(Students should hold their thumbs up.)*

Muéstrenme cómo apuntan su pulgar hacia arriba.

(Monitor, and correct.)

Si no escuchan el sonido /mmm/ al principio de la palabra, entonces apunten su pulgar hacia abajo. *(Demonstrate a thumbs-down.)*

¿Qué van a hacer si no escuchan el sonido /mmm/ al principio de la palabra? *(Students should hold their thumbs down.)*

Muéstrenme cómo apuntan su pulgar hacia abajo.

(Monitor, and correct.)

¡Muy bien!

Mi turno. Primera palabra. *(Pause.)* **/Mmm/ono. ¿Escucho /mmm/ al principio de mono?**

Sí, así que apunto mi pulgar hacia arriba. *(Demonstrate a thumbs-up.)*

Háganlo conmigo. Listos. /Mmm/ono. ¿Escuchamos /mmm/ al principio de /mmm/ono? *(Teacher and students should hold their thumbs up.)*

(Praise students.) **¡Muy bien! Mono comienza con el sonido /mmm/.**

(Monitor, and scaffold as necessary. Emphasize the beginning sound in each word.)

5 Lesson 1

Lesson 1

Ahora todos bajen sus manos.
La siguiente palabra. /Sss/iete.
¿Escuchamos /mmm/ al principio de
/sss/iete?

(Teacher and students should hold their thumbs
down. Monitor.)

Ahora ustedes. ¿Escuchan /mmm/ al
principio de /sss/iete?
(Students should give a thumbs-down.)

**Repeat the process with the following
words: me, mar, va, martes, soy,
mundo, muy.**

(If a student makes a mistake, immediately stop
and use the model-lead-test strategy.)

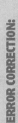

ERROR CORRECTION:
Mi turno. Escuchen nuevamente.
(Repeat the word the student was mistaken
about.)
La palabra es _____. No escucho
/mmm/ al principio de la palabra _____,
así que apunto mi pulgar hacia abajo.
(Demonstrate a thumbs-down.)
Ahora, ustedes juntos. ¿Escuchan
/mmm/ al principio de _____? No.
¿Entonces, qué hacen? (Check to make
sure all thumbs are up or down based on
the word.)
Ahora vamos a hacerlo otra vez. (Back
up 2 items and restart the activity.)

¡Buen trabajo reconociendo la palabra que
comienza con /mmm/ y la palabra que no
comienza con /mmm/!

Individual Practice

(Provide individual practice with 1 or 2 words per
student.)

Terminamos otra actividad. Ahora puedo
marcar la caja para esta actividad en la
Hoja de maestría.

Activity 5
Writing the Letter

(Have the marker board prepared
to demonstrate tracing m twice.
Hold up the **Mm** Tarjeta de
sonido. Touch under m.)

¿Cuál es el sonido de esta
letra? /mmm/
Sí, /mmm/. Vamos a aprender a escribir la
letra que hace el sonido /mmm/. Vamos a
aprender a escribir la letra m.

Observen cómo escribo la letra m. (Model,
explaining each stroke you make. Use the
marker board.) Pongo mi lápiz en el punto
grande. Trazo la letra que hace el sonido
/mmm/. Trazo la letra m.

Vayan a la página 1 en el Libro de
actividades A.

(Direct students to the first m.)

Miren esta página del Libro de
actividades A. Las letras en esta página
están casi escritas.
Pongan su lápiz en el punto grande.
(Demonstrate, and monitor.) Tracen la letra
conmigo mientras dicen /mmm/.

Lesson 1

Note: Verbally walk students through strokes used to trace the letter *m*. Scaffold as necessary. Students must not be left on their own to complete a line of tracing *m*. Direct them to the next *m* to trace and give them specific directions: **Pongan su lápiz en el siguiente punto grande. Tracen la letra mientras dicen /mmm/.** Have students trace all the *m*'s on the first line: **Continúen hasta que hayan trazado todas las letras en el renglón.**

(Monitor, and correct as necessary.)

¡Buen trabajo trazando la letra que hace el sonido /mmm/!

(Direct students to the next line.)

En el siguiente renglón escriban la letra *m*. Escríbanla mientras dicen el sonido /mmm/. *(Monitor, and correct.)*

Note: Scaffold as necessary. Students must not be left on their own to complete a line of writing *m*. Give them specific directions: **Pongan su lápiz en el punto grande. Escriban la letra mientras dicen /mmm/.** Continue the pattern until students have written an *m* for each set of dots on the second line: **Continúen hasta que hayan escrito todas las letras en el renglón.**

¡Buen trabajo escribiendo la letra *m*!

Miren los últimos seis espacios en esta página del *Libro de actividades A*. Ahora, vamos a jugar a un juego. Voy a decir una palabra, y si comienza con el sonido /mmm/, escriban la letra *m* en el primer espacio. *(Demonstrate writing *m* on the marker board.)*

Pongan su lápiz en el primer espacio. *(Monitor, and correct.)*

Escuchen atentamente. *Moto*. *(Pause.)* **/Mmm/oto.**

¿Escuchan /mmm/ al principio de la palabra /mmm/oto? Sí.

Entonces, escriban la letra *m* en el primer espacio.

(Monitor.)

Note: *Moto* has different meanings in different countries.

Siguiente palabra. /Lll/eche.

¿Escuchan /mmm/ al principio de la palabra? No.

¿Escriben la letra *m* en el siguiente espacio? No.

¡Buen trabajo!

(Scaffold as necessary.)

Remind students the sound of the letter m is /mmm/.

Recuerden que el sonido de la letra *m* es /mmm/. ¿Cuál es el sonido de la letra *m*? /mmm/

¡Muy bien!

*(Hold up the **Mm** Tarjeta de sonido. Touch under m in the word mango.)* **¿Cuál es el nombre de esta letra?** m

¡Muy bien! *M* es la primera letra en /mmm/ango y el sonido de *m* es /mmm/.

¿Escuchamos /mmm/ al principio de /lll/eche? No.

¡Buen trabajo! No escuchamos /mmm/ al principio de /lll/eche porque *m* no es la primera letra de *leche*. Ahora, ¿qué hacen cuando escuchan la palabra *leche*? ¿Escriben *m* en el espacio? No. **Muy bien.**

Dejen en blanco el segundo espacio.

Siguiente palabra. /Mmm/ango. ¿Escuchan /mmm/ en la palabra /mmm/ango? Sí.

¡Muy bien! Escriban *m* en el tercer espacio.

(Monitor, and correct if necessary.)

7 Lesson 1

(Students will skip a space for the words that do not begin with /mmm/. There are six spaces for the words.)

Repeat the process with the following words: mercado, millón, sol.

¡Buen trabajo escribiendo la letra *m* para las palabras que comienzan con el sonido /mmm/!

Individual Practice

(Provide individual practice. Help students prepare their own piece of paper by drawing the dots that aid in writing the letter m on the marker board. Demonstrate the use of dots in writing the letter m.)

Han hecho otra parte de la lección perfectamente. Ahora puedo marcar la caja para esta actividad en la Hoja de maestría.

Activity 6
Stretch the Word Game

Note: Remember to hold each continuous sound for about 2 seconds.

Éste es un juego nuevo. Se llama "¡Estirando palabras!". Así es como jugamos "¡Estirando palabras!". Diré una palabra, y me dirán los sonidos que oyen en la palabra o estirarán la palabra. Vamos a aprender cómo estirar palabras. Observen cómo lo hago. Primero levanto mi mano con el puño cerrado. *(Demonstrate.)* **Luego, levanto un dedo por cada sonido de la palabra que estoy diciendo.**

La primera palabra es *mi*. *(Pause.)* **/Mmm/iii/.** *(Demonstrate by raising 1 finger for each sound in mi as you say the sound.)* **¿Ven cómo levanto un dedo por cada sonido que estiro en la palabra *mi*? Háganlo conmigo. Levanten su puño. Estiremos *mi*.** *(Hold up one finger for each sound with students.)* **/mmm/iii/**

(Teacher and students:) /mmm/iii/

(Scaffold as necessary.)

(Remind students the sound of the letter m is /mmm/.)

Recuerden que el sonido de la letra *m* es /mmm/. ¿Cuál es el sonido de la letra *m*? /mmm/

¡Muy bien! *M* es la primera letra de /mmm/i y el sonido de *m* es /mmm/. Ahora, escuchen el siguiente sonido en *mi*. *(Pause.)* **/iii/. La palabra *mi* tiene dos sonidos, /mmm/ e /iii/. /Mmm/iii/.** *(Hold up one finger for each sound.)*

Si estamos levantando nuestros dedos cuando decimos cada sonido de la palabra, ¿qué hacen cuando estiran la palabra *mi*? *(Check each student. Be sure they are correctly holding up one finger for each sound in the word.)*

¡Muy bien!

Siguiente palabra. *Me*. Estiren *me*. /Mmm/eee/. *(Pause. Demonstrate by raising one finger for each sound in me.)* **/mmm/eee/**

(Scaffold as necessary.)

(Repeat until all students can stretch me. If a student makes a mistake, immediately stop and use the model-lead-test strategy.)

ERROR CORRECTION:
Mi turno. Escuchen y miren nuevamente. /Mmm/eee/. *(Pause. Demonstrate by raising one finger for each sound in me.)*
Ahora, háganlo conmigo. /Mmm/eee/. /Mmm/eee/. *(Teacher and students should hold up one finger for each sound as the word is stretched.)* **¡Muy bien!**
Ahora, ustedes juntos. */mmm/eee/.* *(Check each student. Be sure they are correctly holding up one finger for each sound in the word.)*
Ahora vamos a hacerlo otra vez. *(Back up 2 items and restart the activity.)*

Individual Practice

(Provide individual practice.)

¡Buen trabajo! Terminamos esta actividad correctamente. Puedo marcar esta caja en la Hoja de maestría y podemos pasar a la siguiente actividad.

Activity 7
Phonological Awareness
Listening to Syllables

Las palabras se dividen en sílabas. Una sílaba es parte de una palabra. Vamos a escuchar las sílabas de unas palabras. Diré una palabra y todos vamos a dar una palmada por cada sílaba de la palabra que escuchamos.

Mi turno. La palabra es *mamá*. *(Pause. Demonstrate 2 claps while saying:) Ma/má.*

Háganlo conmigo. La palabra es *mamá*. *(Pause. Cue students using the hand-drop cue.) (Teacher and students:) ma (clap) má (clap)*

Ahora ustedes. Digan *mamá* y den una palmada por cada sílaba de la palabra. ma (clap) má (clap)

(Scaffold as necessary.)

ERROR CORRECTION:
(Remind students of how they segmented words into sounds.)
Recuerden cómo estiraron la palabra *mí*. ¿Cómo estiraron la palabra? */mmm/iii/*
(Students should hold up one finger for each sound as they stretch the word.)
¡Muy bien!
Hacemos algo semejante aquí con sílabas. En vez de levantando dedos por cada sonido, estamos dando una palmada por cada sílaba.

Si damos una palmada por cada sílaba cuando decimos la palabra, ¿qué hacen cuando dicen la palabra *mamá*? *(Check each student. Be sure they are correctly clapping for each syllable in the word.)*
¡Muy bien!
(Repeat the procedure until each student understands the procedure.)

Lesson 1

Siguiente palabra.

Repeat the process with the following words: del, sal/sa, me/sa, a/ma, si, po/co, ju/gue/te, e/lla, el.

Individual Practice

(Provide individual practice.)

¡Buen trabajo! Terminamos esta actividad correctamente. Puedo marcar esta caja en la Hoja de maestría y podemos pasar a la siguiente actividad.

Activity 8

Phonological Awareness
Building Syllables

Ahora vamos a formar sílabas. Una sílaba es parte de una palabra. Podemos formar una sílaba cuando juntamos sonidos.

(Hold up the Mm Tarjeta de sonido.)

¿Cuál es el sonido de esta letra? *(Touch under m.)* /mmm/

Mi turno. Escuchen. Si digo /mmm/ y añado /aaa/, se forma la sílaba ma. /Mmm/ y /aaa/ juntos forman ma.

Háganlo conmigo. Si digo /mmm/ y añado /aaa/, ¿qué sílaba se forma? *(Pause 2 seconds. Cue students using the hand-drop cue. Teacher and students:)* ma

Ahora, ustedes solos. /Mmm/. *(Pause.)* **/Aaa/. ¿Qué sílaba se forma?** ma

Siguiente sílaba. Escuchen. /Mmm/. *(Pause.)* **/Eee/. ¿Qué sílaba se forma?** *(Pause 2 seconds.)* me

(If a student makes a mistake, immediately stop and use the model-lead-test strategy.)

ERROR CORRECTION:
Mi turno. Escuchen nuevamente. /Mmm/. *(Pause.)* **/Eee/.** *(Pause)* **Me.**
Ahora, háganlo conmigo. /Mmm/eee/. *(Teacher and students:)* me
¡Muy bien!
Ahora, ustedes juntos. /mmm/eee/ me *(Check each student. Be sure they are correctly forming the syllable.)*
Ahora vamos a hacerlo otra vez. *(Back up 2 items and restart the activity.)*

Individual Practice

(Provide individual practice.)

¡Buen trabajo formando sílabas! Ahora puedo marcar la caja para esta actividad en la Hoja de maestría.

10 Lesson 1

Lesson 1

Activity 9
Oral Blending
Say the Word Game

(Use Pepe the puppet to speak words in stretched form.)

Vamos a jugar a un juego nuevo. Se llama "¡Digan la palabra!". Así es como jugamos "¡Digan la palabra!". Éste es nuestro amigo Pepe. Pepe no puede decir las palabras como nosotros. A él le gusta estirar las palabras lentamente. Cuando Pepe hable, ustedes tienen que escuchar atentamente y decirme qué palabra estiró Pepe.

Voy a decirle una palabra a Pepe y él la estirará. Cuando lo indique, digan la palabra que oyeron.

(Pretend to whisper the word ama to Pepe.)

(Pepe:) **/Aaa/mmm/aaa/.**
(Pause.) **¿Qué palabra estiró Pepe?** *(Cue students using the hand-drop cue.)* **ama**

¡Muy bien! Él dijo *ama*.

Siguiente palabra. Escuchen.

(Move Pepe's mouth as if he were stretching the word. Pepe:) **/Sss/ooo/lll/.**
¿Qué palabra estiró Pepe? *(Cue students using the hand-drop cue.)* **sol**

¡Buen trabajo diciendo la palabra que estiró Pepe!

Listos. Siguiente palabra.

> **Repeat the process with the following words: en, sal, va.**

(Scaffold as necessary.)

Individual Practice

(Provide individual practice with 1 word per student.)

Terminamos esta actividad. Vamos a marcar la Hoja de maestría. Contemos las marcas todos juntos. Al final, indicaremos que hemos terminado la lección.

¡Buen trabajo! Han completado todas las actividades de esta lección y ahora tienen las habilidades que se enseñaron en cada actividad. Ahora Pepe quiere darles un abrazo.

Ya que hemos terminado todas las partes de nuestra lección, puedo poner un adhesivo en la Hoja de maestría de esta lección.

11 Lesson 1

Lección 1

m

Actividad 5

m   m   m   m   m

m   m   m   m   m

m   m

m   m

Lesson 48

MATERIALS

1. *Libro decodificable 13, El pato y el ratón*
2. Timer
3. Marker Board
4. *Libro de actividades B*, pages 14–16
5. Tarjetas de palabras de uso frecuente 18–19
6. *Libro decodificable 14, Mi gato*

OBJECTIVES

Activity 1 *Fluency*
• Decode text and read words fast
• Automatically recognize high-frequency words
• Build fluency by rereading a story in unison

Activity 2 *Comprehension Strategies*
• Identify main characters, setting, problem, and outcome in a selection

Activity 3 *Letter-Sound Correspondences*
• Associate sounds with letters

Activity 4 *Word Recognition and Spelling*
• Learn to write complete sentences

Activity 5 *Word Recognition and Spelling*
• Segment words into syllables, and then blend the syllables to say the words

Activity 6 *Word Recognition and Spelling*
• Internalize sounding-out procedure to become fluent readers

Activity 7 *Word Recognition and Spelling*
• Learn to write and automatically recognize high-frequency words

Activity 8 *Fluency*
• Decode text and read words fast
• Automatically recognize high-frequency words
• Build fluency by reading a story in unison
• Retell a story in order of events

Activity 1
Decodable Book
Fluency Development

(Pass out Libro decodificable 13, El pato y el ratón, to students.)

(You will use a timer and marker board for this activity.)

FLUENCY GOAL 39 words @ 23 words per minute = 1 minute, 50 seconds

Note: Have students read from their books, touching under the words as they read them. Students read fast first the first time in unison. Tap once for each word, allowing enough think time between taps for students to sound out decodable words in their heads.

Vamos a leer el cuento *El pato y el ratón* nuevamente. Lean las palabras rápidamente la primera vez sin decir los sonidos en voz alta.

Pongan el dedo en las palabras. Yo les daré tiempo para decir las palabras en silencio. Luego daré golpecitos en la mesa. Cuando dé un golpecito en la mesa, digan la palabra en voz alta. Pongan el dedo en cada palabra en su libro. *(Monitor.)*

Listos. *(Pause.)*

(Provide think time—3 seconds per word, start timer, and tap.)

Follow the reading format for the entire story.

Note: Follow the usual error correction process for reading activities. Use the marker board to review any missed words.

Individual Practice

(Call on individual students to read 1 or 2 sentences. Monitor to be sure all students are following along. Do not tap during individual practice. Time group reading. Note on the Mastery Sheet whether the group achieved the fluency goal.)

¡Muy bien! **Completaron esta actividad perfectamente. Marcaré esta actividad en la Hoja de maestría.**

47 Lesson 48

Activity 2
Comprehension
Story Grammar

(Write the following words vertically on the marker board: Quién, Problema, Eventos: 1, 2, 3, 4, and Final.)

Vamos a hablar de lo que acabamos de leer. ¿Sobre quién trata el cuento? papá pato

Voy a escribir *papá pato* **al lado de** *Quién* **porque el cuento trata sobre él.** *(Write* papá pato beside Quién.*)*

¿Qué le pasa a papá pato? Se le metió una espina.

¡Muy bien! Voy a escribir *Se le metió una espina* **al lado de** *Problema.*

¿Qué pasa primero? *(Accept reasonable responses such as:* Papá Pato gemía porque se le metió una espina.*)*

¿Qué pasa después? *(Accept reasonable responses such as:* La espina no salía.*)*

¿Qué pasa después? *(Accept reasonable responses such as:* Sale un ratón.*)*

¿Qué pasa después? *(Accept reasonable responses such as:* El ratón le saca la espina [con los colmillos.])*

¿Qué pasa al final del cuento? Papá pato le da de comer al ratón por haberle sacado la espina.

Voy a escribir *Papá pato le da de comer al ratón por haberle sacado la espina al lado de* **Final.**

(Monitor, correct, and scaffold as necessary.)

¡Muy buen trabajo resumiendo el cuento! Ahora puedo marcar la caja para esta actividad en la Hoja de maestría.

Activity 3
Letter-Sound Review

Van a repasar los sonidos de algunas de las letras que hemos aprendido hasta ahora.

(Hold up the book so all students can see the letters. Remember the procedure for letter blends: Touch under the dotted letter and ask for the letter sound. Then slide your finger under the syllable and ask for the syllable sound.)

Ustedes conocen estas letras.

Cuando señale una letra, digan su sonido y continúen diciéndolo hasta que señale la siguiente.

(Touch under the letter V.)
¿Cuál es el sonido? /vvv/

(Scaffold as necessary.)

(Touch under the letter g of gi.)
¿Cuál es el sonido? /j/

(Touch under the syllable gi.)
¿Qué sílaba es? /ji/

v gi ge
v v
ll l v
n gi
Ll ge f
v u
v

Repeat the process with the remaining letters and syllables.

Individual Practice

(Provide individual practice with 2 sounds per student.)

¡Muy buen trabajo diciendo todos los sonidos! Ahora puedo marcar esta actividad en la Hoja de maestría, y podemos pasar a la siguiente actividad.

Lesson 48

Activity 4
Writing the Sentence

Miren las palabras para la actividad 4 en el *Libro de actividades B.*
Prepárense para escribir. Van a escribir una oración. Escúchenla. *Se le metió algo en la pata.*
Escuchen otra vez. *Se le metió algo en la pata.*
Díganla conmigo. Se le metió algo en la pata.
Escriban las palabras de la oración siguiendo el orden en que las escucharon. ¿Con qué tipo de letra debe comenzar una oración? *(Monitor.)* con mayúscula
Escriban la primera letra con mayúscula. Se Siguiente palabra. le

> Repeat the process with the following words: **metió, algo, en, la, pata.**

(Scaffold as necessary.)

Lean la oración que escribieron. Se le metió algo en la pata.
Pongan un punto al final de la oración.
Escriban la oración otra vez en el siguiente renglón.

(Scaffold as necessary.)

¡Excelente trabajo escribiendo la oración! Marcaré esta actividad en la Hoja de maestría.

Dejen el libro de actividades abierto porque lo usaremos más tarde.

50 Lesson 48

Activity 5
Sounding Out
Chunking—Student Led

Miren las palabras para la actividad 5 en el *Libro de actividades B.*
Van a formar palabras multisilábicas. Van a leer cada palabra por sílabas y luego la leerán rápidamente.
Pongan el dedo en la primera palabra. *(Monitor.)*

Lean la sílaba. *(Students should slide a finger under Vic.)* **Vic**
Lean la sílaba. *(Students should slide a finger under tor.)* **tor**
Lean la palabra rápidamente. *(Students should slide a finger under Victor.)* **Victor**

(Scaffold as necessary.)

¡Muy bien!
Siguiente palabra.

> Repeat the process with the following words: **único, contesta, vamos, saluda, verde, lindo, salta, final.**

(Scaffold as necessary.)

(Provide individual practice.)

¡Buen trabajo! Marcaré esta actividad en la Hoja de maestría. ¡Solamente hay unas pocas actividades más y acabaremos la lección!

Dejen el libro de actividades abierto porque lo usaremos más tarde.

Lesson 48

Activity 6
Reading Fast First
Words

Miren las palabras para la actividad 6 en el *Libro de actividades B.*

Van a leer estas palabras rápidamente. Piensen en los sonidos y lean toda la palabra lo más rápidamente que puedan.

Pongan el dedo en la primera palabra. *(Monitor.)* **Listos.**

Piensen. *(Allow 3 seconds of think time.)*
Lean la palabra. *(Students should slide a finger under malo.)* **malo**
(Scaffold as necessary.)

Siguiente palabra.

Piensen. *(Allow 3 seconds of think time.)*
Lean la palabra. *(Students should slide a finger under vivo.)* **vivo**
(Scaffold as necessary.)

Repeat the process with the following words: **lindo, esta, está, estar, sofá, salta, dile, gusta, cola, con, del, algo, ver.**

Individual Practice
(Provide individual practice.)

¡Buen trabajo leyendo las palabras! Marcaré esta actividad en la Hoja de maestría.

Activity 7
High-Frequency Words
New

(Have ready Tarjetas de palabras de uso frecuente 18–19.)

Hoy aprenderemos dos palabras nuevas. **La primera palabra es *arriba.* *(Pause.)* Repítanla conmigo.**
(Teachers and students:) arriba
(Scaffold as necessary.)

Ahora ustedes. *(Hold up Tarjeta de palabra de uso frecuente — arriba.)* **Listos. Lean la palabra. arriba**
(Scaffold as necessary.)

Individual Practice
(Provide individual practice.)

La segunda palabra nueva es *corre.* Repítanla conmigo.
(Teachers and students:) corre
(Scaffold as necessary.)

Ahora ustedes. *(Hold up Tarjeta de palabra de uso frecuente — corre.)* **Listos. Lean la palabra. corre**
(Scaffold as necessary.)

Individual Practice
(Provide individual practice.)

Miren la actividad 7 en el *Libro de actividades B.* Van a escribir las palabras *arriba* y *corre.* Las letras del sonido fuerte /rr/ ya están escritas en el medio de la palabra porque aún no conocen ese sonido. Sólo falta escribir las letras de los demás sonidos. Escuchen la palabra *arriba.* Piensen en los sonidos y escríbanlos en el orden en que los escuchan. *(Allow 3 seconds of think time.)*
(Monitor that each student writes the letters in the correct order.)

¿Qué palabra escribieron? arriba
Siguiente palabra.

Repeat the process with the following word: **corre.**

¡Buen trabajo leyendo y escribiendo las palabras frecuentes! Ahora puedo marcar la Hoja de maestría, y podemos pasar a la siguiente parte de la lección.

Lesson 48

Activity 8
Decodable Book
Fluency Development

(You will use a timer and the marker board for this activity.)

*(Pass out **Libro decodificable 14,** Mi gato, to students.)*

FLUENCY GOAL 82 words @ 24 words per minute = 3 minutes, 30 seconds

Note: Have students read from their own books, touching under the words as they read them. Students read fast first the first time in unison. Tap once for each word, allowing enough think time between taps for students to sound out decodable words in their heads.

Part A: First Reading

(Hold up a copy of Mi Gato, and point to the cover.)

Ahora vamos a leer un cuento nuevo que trata de un gato.

Van a hojear el libro y mirar los dibujos. ¿Qué piensan que va a pasar en el cuento?

(Accept reasonable responses.)

Ahora vamos a leer el cuento *Mi gato* rápidamente desde el principio. Si saben la palabra, díganla cuando dé un golpecito. Si no saben la palabra, díganla por sílabas en silencio, y luego díganla rápidamente en voz alta cuando yo dé un golpecito. Les daré tiempo para pensar antes de que golpee. Pongan el dedo en cada palabra en su libro.

Note: Provide no more than 2.5 seconds maximum think time per word.

Van a leer el título primero. Pongan el dedo en la primera palabra del título y muéstrenme que están listos para leer. *(Monitor.)* **Listos.** *(Pause.)* *(Tap.)* **Mi** *(tap)* **gato**

¡Muy bien! Ahora van a leer todo el cuento. Pongan el dedo en la primera palabra del cuento en la página 3. *(Monitor to verify that all students are touching the correct word.)* **Listos.** *(Pause. Start timer. Tap.)* **A** *(tap)* **mi** *(tap)* **gato**

> Repeat the process with the entire story.

Note: Follow the usual error correction process for reading activities. Use the marker board to review any missed words.

(Check students' predictions:) **¿Acertaron en lo que sucedería en el cuento?** *(Discuss.)*

Part B: Second Reading

Ahora ustedes van a leer el cuento rápidamente sin parar. Listos. *(Tap.)* **A** *(tap)* **mi** *(tap)* **gato**

Note: Provide no more than 2.5 seconds maximum think time per word.

> Repeat the process with the entire story.

Note: Use the marker board to review any missed words.

Individual Practice

(Call on individual students to read 1 or 2 sentences. Monitor to be sure all students are following along. Do not tap during individual practice. Time students as a group. On the Mastery Sheet, note whether the group met the fluency goal.)

Part C: Retell

¿Cómo comienza el cuento? *(Call on students to retell the story in their own words.)*

¡Muy buen trabajo leyendo el cuento! Completaron esta actividad perfectamente. Marcaré la Hoja de maestría. Puedo poner un adhesivo en la Hoja de maestría de esta lección.

Lección 48

Actividad 4

Se le metió algo en la pata.

Se le metió algo en la pata.

Actividad 5

Víctor		único
contesta		vamos
saluda		verde
lindo	salta	final

14

Libro de actividades B

Lección 48

Actividad 6

malo	vivo
lindo	esta
estar	sofá
salta	dile
gusta	cola
con	del
algo	ver

Lección 48

Actividad 7

arriba

corre

16

Libro de actividades B

Lesson 82

MATERIALS

1. *Libro decodificable 37, La araña*
2. Timer
3. Tarjetas de sílabas 1–18
4. *Libro de actividades C,* pages 2–3
5. *Libro decodificable 38, Canta...canta...canta*
6. Marker Board

OBJECTIVES

Activity 1 *Fluency*
- Decode text and read words fast
- Automatically recognize high-frequency words
- Build fluency by rereading a story in unison

Activity 2 *Comprehension Strategies, Word Recognition and Spelling*
- Build fluency by reading a passage and discussing main ideas
- Write main ideas in complete sentences

Activity 3 *Word Recognition and Spelling*
- Learn to automatically recognize syllables

Activity 4 *Word Recognition and Spelling*
- Internalize sounding-out procedure

Activity 5 *Word Recognition and Spelling*
- Segment words into syllables, and then blend the syllables to say the words

Activity 6 *Fluency*
- Decode text and read words fast
- Automatically recognize high-frequency words
- Build fluency by reading a story in unison

Activity 7 *Comprehension Strategies*
- Use a graphic organizer to review information and details from a selection

---

Activity 1
Decodable Book
Fluency Development

(You will use the timer for this activity.)

*(Pass out **Libro decodificable 37**, La araña, to students.)*

FLUENCY GOAL 75 words @ 40 wpm = 2 minutes

Vamos a leer el cuento *La araña* nuevamente. Lean las palabras rápidamente la primera vez sin decir los sonidos en voz alta. Pongan el dedo en las palabras. Yo les daré tiempo para decir las palabras en silencio. Luego daré golpecitos en la mesa. Cuando dé un golpecito en la mesa, digan la palabra en voz alta.

Note: Provide no more than 1.5 seconds maximum think time per word.

Prepárense para leer. Pongan el dedo bajo la primera palabra.

(Pause, start the timer, and tap.)

Repeat the process for the entire story.

Note: Review any missed words. If students met the fluency goal on the first reading in this lesson, have them move to Individual Practice. If students did not meet the fluency goal on the first reading, have students read the story a second time in unison. This time have them read the story faster, pausing 1.5 seconds maximum for think time per word. Then have students complete Individual Practice.

Ahora lean el cuento nuevamente. Veamos si pueden leerlo un poco más rápidamente esta vez. Listos.

(Pause, start the timer, and tap.)

Note: Review any missed words.

Individual Practice

(Call on individual students to read 1 or 2 pages. Do not tap during individual reading. Time students as a group. Note on the Mastery Sheet whether the group met the fluency goal.)

¡Buen trabajo leyendo este cuento! Completaron esta actividad perfectamente. Ahora puedo marcar la caja para esta actividad en la Hoja de maestría.

Lesson 82

Activity 2
Main Idea
Sentence Dictation

Ahora que leyeron *La araña*, díganme: ¿cuál es la idea principal del cuento? La telaraña de Fili es toda su vida.

(Scaffold as necessary.)

¿Qué le pasó a la araña? El balón dañó su tela. Sí, eso pasó. ¿Qué más? La araña teje otra tela en lo alto de un árbol.

Muy bien.

Miren los espacios para la actividad 2 en la página 2 del *Libro de actividades C*.

Vamos a escribir la idea principal en una oración.

Escuchen. La idea principal es *La telaraña de Fili es toda su vida.*

Esta oración es la idea principal del cuento. Repítanla conmigo.

(Teacher and students:) **La telaraña de Fili es toda su vida.**

Ahora van a escribirla. ¿Qué ponemos al final de una oración? un punto

Muy bien.

(Praise those who remembered. Scaffold those who forgot.)

Repitan la oración solos. La telaraña de Fili es toda su vida.

Ahora escríbanla en sus cuadernos en el orden en que la dijeron.

¡Excelente! Hemos terminado otra actividad, y puedo marcar la caja para esta actividad en la Hoja de maestría.

Dejen el libro de actividades abierto porque lo usaremos más tarde.

Lesson 82

Activity 4
Reading Fast First
Words

Miren las palabras para la actividad 4 en el *Libro de actividades C.*

Van a leer las palabras rápidamente. Pongan el dedo debajo de la primera palabra. *(Monitor.)*

Listos.
Piensen. *(Allow 1 second of think time.)*
Lean la palabra. baño
(Slide your finger under baño.) baño

(Scaffold as necessary.)

Siguiente palabra.

Piensen. *(Allow 1 second of think time.)*
Lean la palabra. *(Slide your finger under noche.)* noche

(Scaffold as necessary.)

Repeat the process with the following words: **canta, ocho, casa, año, techo, coche, plaza.**

Ahora van a leer más rápidamente las mismas palabras. Pongan el dedo en la primera palabra.

Listos. *(Allow 1 second of think time.)*
Lean la palabra. baño

Siguiente palabra.

Repeat the process with the remaining words.

Individual Practice

(Provide individual practice, having each student read the entire word list as fast as possible.)

(Scaffold as necessary.)

¡Buen trabajo leyendo las palabras! Marcaré esta actividad en la Hoja de maestría, y podemos pasar a la siguiente actividad.

Dejen el libro de actividades abierto porque lo usaremos más tarde.

Activity 5
Sounding Out
Chunking—Student Led

Pasen a la página 3 en el *Libro de actividades C.*

Ahora van a formar palabras multisilábicas. Van a leer cada palabra por sílabas y luego la van a leer rápidamente. Pongan el dedo en la primera palabra.

Lean la sílaba. *(Students should slide a finger under mú.)* mú
Lean la sílaba. *(Students should slide a finger under si.)* si
Lean la sílaba. *(Students should slide a finger under ca.)* ca
Léan la palabra rápidamente. *(Students should quickly slide a finger under the entire word.)* música

¡Muy bien!
Siguiente palabra.

Repeat the process with the following words: **entrada, muchacho, ratones, zapato, gemían.**

Individual Practice

(Provide individual practice.)

¡Buen trabajo! Marcaré esta actividad en la Hoja de maestría.

Lesson 82

Activity 7
Comprehension
Content Web

(You will need the marker board for this activity. You will create a content web on the marker board.)

Vamos a hablar de lo que hemos leído. Vamos a hacer un diagrama de red acerca del cuento. Sin mirar sus cuentos, nombren los personajes a quienes les gusta cantar.

(Continue asking: ¿A quién le gusta cantar? until all the characters have been named. Accept answers such as el joven, el loro, la mamá, el papá.)

(Draw a main circle on the marker board.)

En el medio de la red, vamos a escribir Les gusta cantar.

¿Qué le gusta hacer al joven, al loro, a la mamá, al papá, al gato, al perro y a todos los demás? A todos les gusta cantar.

(Write el joven, el loro, el papá, la mamá, el gato, el perro on the lines coming out from the content web.)

¡Muy bien! Completaron esta actividad perfectamente. Marcaré esta actividad en la Hoja de maestría, y puedo poner un adhesivo en la Hoja de maestría de esta lección.

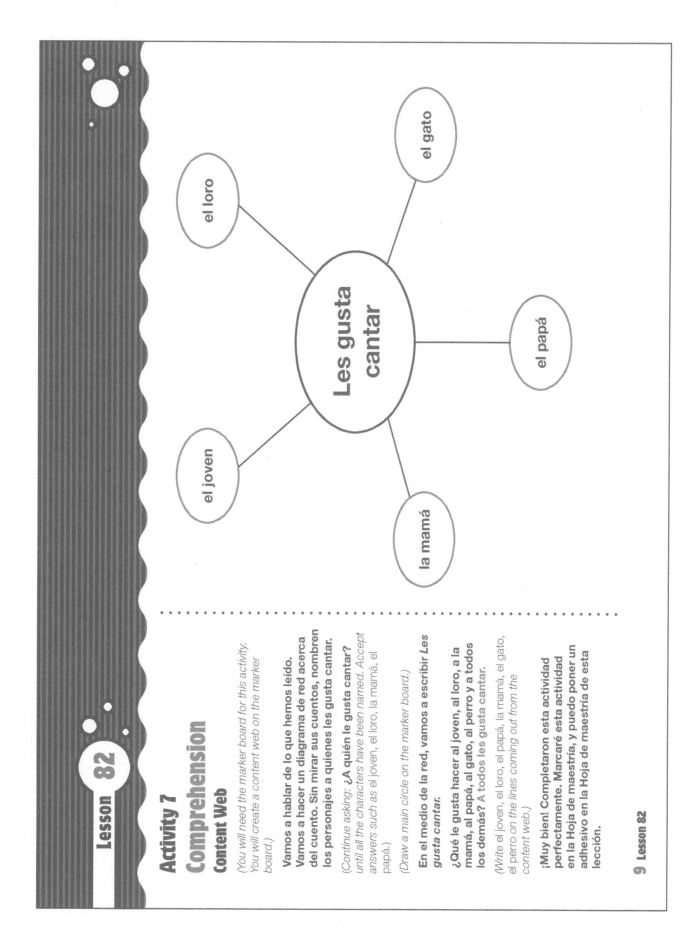

9 Lesson 82

Staff Development Guide, Spanish

183

Lección 82

Actividad 2

La telaraña de Fili es toda su vida.

Actividad 4

baño	noche	canta
ocho	casa	año
techo	coche	plaza

Libro de actividades C

Lección 82

Actividad 5

<u>mú</u><u>si</u><u>ca</u>   <u>en</u><u>tra</u><u>da</u>

<u>mu</u><u>cha</u><u>cho</u>   <u>ra</u><u>to</u><u>nes</u>

<u>za</u><u>pa</u><u>to</u>   <u>ge</u><u>mí</u><u>an</u>

Libro de actividades C   3

Troubleshooting

Problem: Students do not respond on cue.

Solution: Remind students to answer together on cue. If the problem persists, discuss the importance of responding on cue. Remind students that answering together gives them all the opportunity to answer each question. Model the correct way to answer on cue, and practice it with your students. The best way to make sure students continue to answer on cue is to make sure they do it every time.

Problem: One student answers before the cue.

Solution: Validate the student for knowing the answer. Enlist the student to be your helper. Explain how helping means answering on cue. Review the importance of the group answering together. If a student seems to want individual attention, remind the student that everyone has the opportunity to answer by themselves during individual practice.

Problem: A student answers slightly behind the cue.

Solution: Praise the students who responded on cue. When a student answers slightly behind the cue, it usually means he or she does not really know the answer. Treat this as a normal error, and correct it with the Model-Lead-Test strategy. If a student consistently answers behind the cue, increase the think time between cues.

Problem: A student does not hold a continuous sound or mispronounces a sound.

Solution: Mispronouncing sounds causes problems for students when they are decoding and spelling words. Correct the mispronunciation with the Model-Lead-Test strategy. Model the correct way to say the sound. Have students say the sound in unison with you. Then have students say the sound without you. Back up two items and begin the task again.

Problem: Students do not respond on cue.

Solution: Remind students to answer together on cue. If the problem persists, discuss the importance of responding on cue. Remind students that answering together gives them all the opportunity to answer each question. Model the correct way to answer on cue and practice it with your students. The best way to make sure students continue to answer on cue is to make sure they do it every time.

Problem: One student in a group is having difficulty keeping up with the other students.

Solution: Provide a few minutes of one-on-one instruction. Integrate easier items into activities to ensure that the struggling student feels successful. If necessary, regroup the students.

Problem: A student refuses to work.

Solution: A student may be reluctant to work at first because he or she is unsure of what is expected, may not know the answer, or may be afraid to make a mistake. Create a positive, nurturing environment. Add external motivators such as stickers. Play the Beat the Teacher Game in which students get a point for every time they follow directions. However, if everyone in the group does not follow directions, you get a point.

Problem: You find yourself telling one student to sit up and another student to listen.

Solution: Reestablish rules. Examine your pacing. You may be too slow or inconsistent.

Glossary

Alphabetic Pertaining to a writing system that uses a symbol for each speech sound of the language. Of, relating to, or expressed by an alphabet.

Alphabetic Principle Use of letters and letter combinations to represent phonemes in an orthography. Refers to the fact that each sound has a graphic representation.

Blending Auditory skill that increases phonological awareness of the sound structure of words. After a word is stretched by the teacher, the students are asked to put the sounds together and say the word at a normal rate. For example, the teacher says /sss/aaa/lll/, and the students say *sal*. Blending allows the students an extended period of time to hear the smaller units of sound contained in a word. Blending is also referred to as "telescoping a word."

Co-articulated Spoken together so that separate segments are not easily detected.

Comprehension Mental act of knowing when one does and does not understand what one is reading.

Consonant Phoneme that is not a vowel and is formed with obstruction of the flow of air with the teeth, lips, or tongue.

Consonant Blend A combination of two or more distinguishable consonant sounds before or after a vowel. Examples: *cr, dr, tr, bl.*

Consonant Digraph Written letter combination that corresponds to one speech sound but is not represented by either letter alone. Examples: *ch, ll, rr.*

Continuous Sound Letter-sound that can be held without distorting the sound. Examples: *a, e, f, i, l, m, n, o, r, s, u, v, w, y, z.*

Decodable Text Text in which a large proportion of the words (70 to 80 percent) is made up of letter-sound relationships that have already been taught.

Decoding Ability to translate a word from print to speech. The act of deciphering a new word by sounding it out.

Decoding Units Distinct parts that text can be broken into, including letter-sounds, words, phrases, and sentences.

Digraphs Two or three consecutive letters that represent one sound. There are both vowel digraphs and consonant digraphs. Examples: *ch, ll, rr.*

Diphthong Complex speech sound that begins with one vowel sound and gradually changes to another vowel sound within the same syllable. Examples: *ai* in *baile* and *ie* in *cielo.*

Flex Word Word that almost sounds out in a familiar way. Most of the letters in a flex word represent their most common sounds. The word sounds out closely enough that the students can figure out the correct pronunciation.

Grapheme Letter or letter combination that spells a single phoneme. In Spanish a grapheme may be 1, 2, or 3 letters such as *i, ia, iai.*

High-Frequency Words Words taught as whole words until the letter-sound combination is taught. Students need these words in order to read or comprehend text.

Multisyllabic Having more than one syllable.

Orthography Writing system.

Phoneme Speech sound that combines with others in a language system to make words; the smallest phonetic unit in a language that is capable of conveying a distinction in meaning.

Phoneme Awareness (or Phonemic Awareness) The conscious awareness that words are made up of segments of our own speech and are represented with letters in an alphabetic orthography.

Phonics Study of the relationships between letters and the sounds they represent; sound-symbol correspondences. Refers to the system by which symbols represent sounds in an alphabetic writing system.

Phonological Awareness Conscious awareness and knowledge that words are composed of separate sounds or phonemes. Ability to manipulate these phonemes in words.

Phonology Rule system within a language by which phonemes are sequenced and uttered to make words; study of the unconscious rules, which govern speech-sound production.

r-controlled Pertaining to a vowel immediately followed by the consonant *r,* such that its pronunciation is affected, or even dominated, by the /r/ sound.

Reading Fluency Speed of reading, including effortless, accurate, and smooth reading with expression.

Schwa Nondistinct vowel found in unstressed syllables in English.

Scope and Sequence The "scope" refers to the amount or range of information contained in the curriculum. "Sequence" is the order in which the information and/or skills are presented.

Segmenting Auditory skill that helps the students hear the discrete sounds within a word. The teacher says the word at a normal rate, and students are asked to segment it into its individual phonemes. Each continuous sound in a word is held for two seconds, switching from sound to sound without pausing. Stop sounds within the word are said quickly so as not to distort their sound. Segmenting is also referred to as "stretching a word."

Sounding Out Matching a letter-sound to its graphic representation. Starting at the beginning of the word, the students say the sound corresponding to the first letter. Students advance in a left-to-right progression, saying the sound for each successive letter. The sounds are said one after another without stopping between the sounds.

Stop Sounds Consonant speech sound that is articulated with a stop of the airstream. The sound cannot be held without distortion. Examples: *b, c, d, j, k, p, q, t.*

Stretch and Blend Phonological awareness activity that requires students to combine the blending and segmenting exercises. The teacher says a word at the normal rate; the students stretch the word into its individual phonemes and then say the word at the normal rate.

Syllable Unit of pronunciation that is organized around a vowel. It may or may not have consonants before or after the vowel.

Tricky Words (Sight Words) Words that are taught as whole words and are explained as not following the regular sound-spelling rules.

Unstressed Unaccented syllable within a word.

Voiced Speech sound articulated with vibrating vocal cords.

Vowel Open phoneme that is the nucleus of every syllable and is classified by tongue position and height, such as high/low or front/mid/back. Spanish has 5 vowel phonemes.